מגילת אסתר

THE ISRAEL BIBLE
™

SCROLL OF ESTHER

Illustrated by Esther Horgen z"l
Introduction by Benjamin Horgen
Edited by Rabbi Tuly Weisz

The Israel Bible Scroll of Esther
מגילת אסתר
First Edition, 2021

Israel365
www.Israel365.com

The Israel Bible Scroll of Esther was produced and published
by Israel365 and Teach for Israel.
All rights reserved.

No part of this publication may be reproduced, stored in a retrieval system or
transmitted in any for or by any means, electronic, mechanical, photocopying,
or otherwise, without the prior permission of the publisher, except in the
case of brief quotations embedded in critical articles or reviews.

ISBN: 978-1-7333010-2-2 *hardcover*
ISBN: 978-1-7333-0103-9 *paperback*

The Israel Bible Scroll of Esther is a holy book that contains the
name of God and should be treated with respect.

RAPHAËL & NATALIE
Graphic design by Natalie Friedemann-Weinberg
Typography by Raphaël Freeman MISTD, Renana Typesetting

Printed in the United States

It is with profound sadness that
The Israel Bible Scroll of Esther
is dedicated in loving memory of

Esther Horgen
אסתר בת יצחק וקולט הורגן הי"ד

May 28, 1968 – December 20, 2020
א' סיון תשכ"ח – ה' טבת תשפ"א

"And Esther found favor in the eyes of all who saw her…
and Esther was taken before the King in the month of *Tevet*."
(SCROLL OF ESTHER, CHAPTER 2)

וַתְּהִי אֶסְתֵּר נֹשֵׂאת חֵן בְּעֵינֵי כָּל־רֹאֶיהָ
וַתִּלָּקַח אֶסְתֵּר אֶל־הַמֶּלֶךְ בַּחֹדֶשׁ טֵבֵת.
מגילת אסתר ב'

CONTENTS

Letter from Prime Minister Benjamin Netanyahu	vi
Letter from President Rivlin	viii
Introduction by Benjamin Horgen	ix
Foreword by Rabbi Tuly Weisz	xiii
Chapter 1	1
Chapter 2	9
Chapter 3	17
Chapter 4	25
Chapter 5	31
Chapter 6	37
Chapter 7	43
Chapter 8	49
Chapter 9	57
Chapter 10	67
"Fear" by Esther Horgen	71
"La Peur" par Esther Horgen	75
Queen Esther. Chana Senesh. Anne Frank. Esther Horgen	78
Historical Background to the Purim Story	82
Prophets and Prophetesses of the Hebrew Bible	85
Notes on Translation and Transliterated Words	88
The Hebrew Months and their Holidays	91
Map of the Empire of Ahasuerus	94
Map of Modern Day Israel and its Neighbors	95
Prayer for the State of Israel	96
Prayer for the Welfare of Israel's Soldiers	100
Hatikvah	102
About Rabbi Tuly Weisz and Israel365	103
The Esther Horgen Memorial Forest and Park	105

ראש הממשלה
PRIME MINISTER

ירושלים, ב' אדר תשפ"א
14 פברואר 2021

לכבוד
משפחת הורגן

משפחת הורגן היקרה,

קריאת מגילת אסתר בחג הפורים מפגישה אותנו עם יסודות קיומו של עם ישראל לאורך הדורות. בגלות מרחפת מעלינו סכנת הכחדה. תחת חסותו של שליט הפכפך, המלך אחשוורוש, רוקם צורר היהודים המן תכנית השמדה שנועדה להרוג ולאבד את בני עמנו בממלכת פרס ומדי.

זהו ביטוי מובהק לשורשיה הקדומים של האנטישמיות. רעל השנאה מתפשט, ובאין סכר ומעצור הוא מעמיד אותנו בפני איום קיומי. שנאת ישראל עברה מן הזמן העתיק אל ימי-הביניים, ומהם אל הזמן החדש. זוועות אושוויץ וטרבלינקה נבעו מאותו מקור ממש של שטנה הרסנית, חסרת מעצורים – וגם כיום יש מי שמאיים עלינו בחורבן ובהשמדה.

אלא שמגילת אסתר מלמדת אותנו דבר חשוב נוסף: בזכות האמונה בנצח ישראל פורצים מתוכנו כוחות אדירים להשיב מלחמה-שערה לאויבינו. מנהיגותם של מרדכי ואסתר היא מופת של נחישות, תושייה וגאווה לאומית. אסתר אומרת למרדכי 'לך כנוס את כל היהודים'. אחדות האומה היא המפתח להצלחת המאבק בגזרת המן, ולניצחון על מבקשי נפשנו.

אסתר המלכה נשאה חן בעיני כל רואיה, וכמוה אסתר הורגן ז"ל שנלקחה מאיתנו לפני שבועות אחדים בפיגוע טרור נורא. היא הייתה אשת משפחה אוהבת – בת נאמנה, אחות קרובה, רעיה מסורה, אם נפלאה וסבתא מלאת אושר. כל מי שזכה להכיר את אסתר הוקסם מעולמה הפנימי העשיר ומיכולת הנתינה שלה לאחרים.

עלייתה של אסתר מצרפת לישראל הובילה אותה אל היישוב טל מנשה בצפון השומרון. שם בחרה להקים את ביתה, ושם עסקה בייעוץ זוגי ברוח הפסיכולוגיה היהודית. לדאבון לבנו, שם – בלב חורשה מלבלבת, לא רחוק מן הבית – נגדעו חייה בידי בן עוולה. אבל כפי שנאמר במגילה – 'לַיְּהוּדִים הָיְתָה אוֹרָה'; האור המיוחד של אסתר לא יכבה. נגשים את שאיפתה להיאחז במולדתנו ולהעמיק שורש באדמתנו.

אני מברך על היוזמה להוציא לאור את 'מגילת אסתר הורגן' לחג הפורים. המגילה, שמעוטרת באיוריה המרהיבים של אסתר, תשמש נר-תמיד לזכרה.

בברכה,
בנימין נתניהו

Jerusalem, Israel

ראש הממשלה
PRIME MINISTER

Dear Horgen Family,

Reading the Scroll of Esther on Purim connects us with the foundations of the Jewish People throughout the generations. In exile, the dangers of annihilation hung over our heads. Under the reign of King Ahaseurus, the evil Haman arose to murder our people in the empire of Persia and Media.

This is a vivid expression of classic anti-Semitism. The spread of this poisonous hatred with nothing to stop it, is an existential threat to our existence. The hatred of Israel continued from ancient times to the Middle Ages and throughout modern times. The tragedy of Auschwitz and Treblinka came from this unbridled evil, with nothing to prevent its spread. And still today, there are those that threaten us with total destruction.

The Scroll of Esther teaches us something very important: thanks to our faith in Israel's eternity, we can summon unparalleled strength to respond to our enemies' aggression. Mordechai and Esther led with unparalleled determination, heroism and national pride. Esther told Mordechai, "Go, gather all the Jews" (4:16) for unity was the key to defeating Haman's decree, and for victory over all those who seek our destruction.

Queen Esther found favor in the eyes of all who saw her. And so too, Esther Horgen z"l, who was taken from us in recent weeks in a horrific terror attack. She was a faithful wife, cherished daughter, loyal sister, and beloved mother and grandmother, always full of joy. Everyone who had the honor of meeting Esther was impressed with her rich inner world and her generosity towards other people.

Esther made Aliyah from France to Tal Menashe in Northern Samaria where she established a home and worked as a marriage therapist in the spirit of Jewish psychology. With profound sorrow, her life was cut short by a horrible monster in the heart of the forest, not far from her home. However, as it says in the Megillah, "For the Jews there was light" (8:16) and the unique light of Esther Horgen will not be extinguished. We will fulfill her desire to strengthen our homeland and deepen our roots in our soil.

I bless the initiative to publish "Megillat Esther Horgen" for the holiday of Purim. May this Megillah which was designed with Esther's beautiful artwork, serve as an eternal light for her memory.

With Blessings,

Benjamin Netanyahu

February 14, 2021 / Adar 2, 5781
Jerusalem, Israel

Translated from Hebrew by the editor

THE PRESIDENT

Jerusalem, January 28, 2021

Dear Horgen family, Dear friends,

I join with you in celebrating the life of Esther ז״ל in this new edition of Megillat Esther with her own, beautiful illustrations.

How bitter-sweet to celebrate Purim, when we read the story of the triumph of Queen Esther over the wicked plans of Ahasuerus and his advisor the evil Haman to annihilate the Jewish people, when we are mourning the loss of dear Esther.

Purim, whose date was chosen at random by the drawing of lots, reminds us of the unpredictable and indiscriminate hatred that we still face.

And, at the same time, Purim tells us that the noble and brave acts of Esther and Mordechai saved the Jewish people from Haman's plot, and the customs of sharing gifts with friend and with those in need remind us of the strength we derive from our community of family and friends, and our commitment to the common good. These are values that inspired Esther's life - even in the face of those who seek our harm.

In Esther's ז״ל own prescient words, "Fear reflects our lack of faith in ourselves, in life, in G-d. …Terrorism is the result of a fanatical idea taken to the extreme. … If terrorism, then, imposes its hatred and violence on humanity, let us offer love and kindness. … Joy, altruism, and faith that light is more powerful than darkness, that love wins over hatred and that joy overcomes mourning".

May the memory of Esther ז״ל be a blessing, forever engraved in the hearts of the nation.

From Jerusalem,

Reuven (Ruvi) Rivlin

INTRODUCTION
Benjamin Horgen

Esther and Benjamin Horgen

IT IS IMPOSSIBLE TO SUMMARIZE ANY PERSON IN A FEW SENtences, much less such a complete and deep personality as my beloved Esther was.

A caring daughter, a cherished sister, the dedicated mother of our six children, the iconic grandmother of Ofek and Inbar, and last, but not least, my loving wife for more than 30 years.

But above all Esther was herself.

Full of life, lover of life – in all its expressions.

My Esther was blessed with a rare quality – she saw the good in everyone, every place and every moment. She was a deeply spiritual person, who like the Jewish Sages whose teachings had a profound influence upon her, viewed the world in three realms: Olam, Shana and Nefesh, which I will explain.

"Olam" in Hebrew means 'the world' and represents physical space. Esther loved to travel everywhere possible and explore new territories. Obviously, she cherished the Land of Israel and wanted to walk through all its paths, climb all its hills and visit all its cities and villages. A perfect day would be to climb 'the Sartaba' not far from our home before dawn to see the sunrise from the Jordan valley, eat lunch under the shadows of Jerusalem's walls, and sit on the beaches of Tel Aviv to look at the sun disappear into the Mediterranean Sea.

But Esther also wanted to see the entire world! She never missed an occasion to visit a new country. From Australia to Ireland, Sweden to India, Hungary to Brazil and many, many more, she loved every place and marveled at the beauties of this world with an infinite appetite.

"Shana" means 'year' and represents time. Esther and I met when we were 21 and married just a few months later. During these last 30 years, we grew up together and journeyed as one through the cycles of life, births and brits, infant care until Bar and Bat Mitzvahs, birthdays and anniversaries, school graduations and weddings, and even funerals and shivas.

For Esther, any event is an opportunity to manifest love and care for all, to prepare for, live through, and then to remember. The Jewish Calendar paces the life of every Jew, Shabbat after Shabbat, with the Holidays being the highlights of the year.

Like everyone, Esther had her favorite holidays. Unusually, she especially loved Yom Kippur as she was very spiritual in nature. Unsurprisingly, she also loved Purim for its inherent joy of life, and its social dimension. We always hosted the festive Purim feast at our home from noon until late in the evening with many good friends, and of course, plenty of good wine!

These two dates are curiously related: Purim and Yom Kippur, which is known as "Yom Kippurim", 'the day which is akin to Purim'. This connection reveals that the same lofty spiritual level can, and should, be reached on these two occasions: one by fasting, and one by feasting.

"Nefesh" means 'soul' and represents people. Esther loved every person, every human being, and saw the good – and only the good – in everyone. Even when that good was buried very deep inside. It was this love for people that led Esther to be a passionate and successful therapist, helping many to recognize their own value, cherish it and make it blossom.

Esther's interpersonal skills and her "Ayin Tova", her 'good eye,' caused her to see people in two categories: current friends and future friends. In that way, she was just like Queen Esther about whom the Scroll of Esther so accurately states, *"Esther* won the admiration of all who saw her" (2:15).

Forever, I will read the Scroll of Esther with sadness, and the following verse with a special trepidation: 'And *Esther* was taken to the King, in his royal palace, in the tenth month, which is the month of *Tevet*' (2:16). Esther was taken from us to the Royal Palace of the King of Kings on the 5th of *Tevet*, 5781.

As the tragic abduction of Queen Esther led to the salvation of the entire Nation of Israel in the Scroll of Esther, we believe that my Esther's fate is also the harbinger for future blessings and ultimate goodness for the Jewish people and all of humanity.

May her soul be bound in the eternal bonds of life.

תהא נשמתה צרורה בצרור החיים

BENJAMIN HORGEN
Tal Menashe, Israel
Adar 5781 / February 2021

FOREWORD
Rabbi Tuly Weisz

Esther Horgen, a proud Jew in her beloved homeland

THE SCROLL OF ESTHER, OR *MEGILLAT ESTHER*, TELLS THE well-known story of the Jewish community living in exile, threatened by an evil enemy who wanted to annihilate every man, woman and child. Although hidden in the background, God, *Hashem,* the King of Kings, arranged for a special woman to play a pivotal role in saving her people.

During this time of paralyzing fear, Queen Esther recognized that she was called "for such a time as this" to save her brothers and sisters. Esther found courage and wisdom to rise up on behalf of her nation in the face of a vicious enemy. The tale of Esther's bravery is recounted in *Megillat Esther* and has inspired generations.

Thousands of years, and countless persecutions later, the Jewish people have started to return from exile to their ancestral homeland, as promised in the Bible. Incredible miracles have been performed by

the King of Kings, who still prefers to operate from behind the scenes. As a result, not all recognize the Divine hand orchestrating events, and there are still in our generation vile enemies hatching plots to annihilate Jewish men, women and children. To this very day, Jewish blood continues to be shed in the Land of Israel, by our enemies who hate what our return to our homeland represents.

The Israel Bible Scroll of Esther is dedicated to the memory of another special Esther who arose at a time of peril and danger on behalf of her people. Unlike the Purim story, however, Esther Horgen was unable to escape from the murderous enemy. Our Esther was killed *Al Kiddush Hashem*, in sanctification of God's name, brutally murdered for being a proud Jew in her land.

Esther Horgen left a tremendous legacy through her family, her actions, her words and her artwork. These all came together in *The Israel Bible Scroll of Esther* featuring her beautiful illustrations, her poetic messages of hope and faith, and tales of her life and death to inspire another generation. *The Israel Bible* is honored to have collaborated with the Horgen family to bring Esther's artwork to life in this volume.

The Israel Bible is the world's first study bible highlighting the special relationship between the Land and People of Israel. While our team of scholars are all Orthodox Israeli Jews, our readers include many non-Jews who love Israel and who are eager to study *Torah* from a Jewish perspective. It is our goal to fulfill our people's historic mandate to be a "light unto the nations" and to bring about the prophecy:

> "In the days to come, the Mount of *Hashem*'s house shall stand firm above the mountains and tower above the hills; and all the nations shall gaze on it with joy. And the many peoples shall go and say: 'Come, let us go up to the Mount of *Hashem*, to the House of the God of *Yaakov*; that He may instruct us in His ways, and that we may walk in His paths.' For instruction shall come forth from *Tzion*, the word of *Hashem* from *Yerushalayim*." (Isaiah 2:2,3)

This volume would not have been possible without the dedicated staff of Israel365 and the scholars of *The Israel Bible*. I would especially like to thank Shira Shechter, Bracha Sendic, Batya Markowitz and Rabbi Mordechai Gershon for working so quickly and diligently. Thanks also to Raphaël Freeman and Natalie Friedemann-Weinberg for their beautiful design that serves as such a fitting tribute.

By reading, studying and praying over *The Israel Bible Scroll of Esther*, we celebrate Queen Esther and mourn for Esther Horgen, keeping her memory alive so that her death is not in vain.

Rabbi Tuly Weisz
Ramat Beit Shemesh, Israel
Adar 5781 / February 2021

Blessings recited before the reading of *Megillat Esther:*

| Blessed are you, *Hashem* Our God, King of the universe Who has sanctified us with His commandments and commanded us regarding the reading of the *Megillah*. | ba-RUKH a-TAH a-do-NAI e-lo-HAY-nu ME-lekh ha-o-LAM a-SHER ki-d'-SHA-nu b'-mitz-vo-TAV v'-tzi-VA-nu al mik-RA m'-gi-LAH. | בָּרוּךְ אַתָּה יְיָ אֱלֹהֵינוּ מֶלֶךְ הָעוֹלָם אֲשֶׁר קִדְּשָׁנוּ בְּמִצְוֹתָיו וְצִוָּנוּ עַל מִקְרָא מְגִלָּה. |

Blessed are you, *Hashem* Our God, King of the universe Who has performed miracles for our ancestors in those days at this time.

ba-RUKH a-TAH a-do-NAI e-lo-HAY-nu ME-lekh ha-o-LAM she-a-SAH ni-SEEM la-a-vo-TAY-nu ba-ya-MEEM ha-HAYM ba-z'-MAN ha-ZEH

בָּרוּךְ אַתָּה יְיָ אֱלֹהֵינוּ מֶלֶךְ הָעוֹלָם שֶׁעָשָׂה נִסִּים לַאֲבוֹתֵינוּ בַּיָּמִים הָהֵם בַּזְּמַן הַזֶּה.

Blessing recited after reading *Megillat Esther:*

Blessed are you, *Hashem* Our God, King of the universe, Who takes up our grievances, Who judges our claims, Who avenges our wrongs, Who brings retribution upon our enemies and Who exacts vengeance for us from our foes. Blessed are you *Hashem*, who exacts vengeance for His nation Israel from all their foes, the God of salvation.	ba-RUKH a-TAH a-do-NAI e-lo-HAY-nu ME-lekh ha-o-LAM ha-RAV et ree-VAY-nu v'-ha-DAN et dee-NAY-nu v'-ha-no-KAYM et nik-ma-TAY-nu v'-ham-sha-LAYM g'-MUL l'-KHOL o-y'-VAY naf-SHAY-nu v'-ha-nif-RA LA-nu mi-tza-RAY-nu ba-RUKH a-TAH a-do-NAI ha-nif-RA l'-a-MO yis-ra-AYL mi-KOL tza-ray-HEM ha-AYL ha-mo-SHEE-a	בָּרוּךְ אַתָּה יְיָ אֱלֹהֵינוּ מֶלֶךְ הָעוֹלָם הָרָב אֶת רִיבֵנוּ וְהַדָּן אֶת דִּינֵנוּ וְהַנּוֹקֵם אֶת נִקְמָתֵנוּ וְהַמְשַׁלֵּם גְּמוּל לְכָל אוֹיְבֵי נַפְשֵׁנוּ וְהַנִּפְרָע לָנוּ מִצָּרֵינוּ. בָּרוּךְ אַתָּה יְיָ הַנִּפְרָע לְעַמּוֹ יִשְׂרָאֵל מִכָּל צָרֵיהֶם הָאֵל הַמּוֹשִׁיעַ.

CHAPTER 1
פרק א

CHAPTER 1

AHASUERUS, THE PERSIAN KING WHO RULES OVER 127 provinces, hosts a 180-day feast for the elite of his empire in which he flaunts his wealth. Afterwards, he hosts an additional seven-day party for the citizens of his capital, Shushan. As wine flows freely, Ahasuerus becomes duly intoxicated and orders that Vashti, his queen, be brought to his party so that he could show off her beauty before his guests. Vashti refuses to come and Ahasuerus becomes furious. He asks for advice on how to handle Vashti's disobedience. His advisor, Memucan, posits that Vashti's refusal is not only a personal affront to the king but also a national offense, as it will cause a national insurrection of women against their husbands. Memucan suggests that Vashti no longer be allowed to appear before the king, and that her position be given to a more deserving woman. Everyone agrees, and a message is sent throughout the empire that each man should be the master in his home.

1 And it was in the days of Ahasuerus, the Ahasuerus who reigned from India to Ethiopia, an empire of one hundred and twenty-seven provinces.

א וַיְהִי בִּימֵי אֲחַשְׁוֵרוֹשׁ הוּא אֲחַשְׁוֵרוֹשׁ הַמֹּלֵךְ מֵהֹדּוּ וְעַד־כּוּשׁ שֶׁבַע וְעֶשְׂרִים וּמֵאָה מְדִינָה:

2 In those days, when King Ahasuerus sat on the throne of his kingdom, which was in Shushan the capital,

ב בַּיָּמִים הָהֵם כְּשֶׁבֶת הַמֶּלֶךְ אֲחַשְׁוֵרוֹשׁ עַל כִּסֵּא מַלְכוּתוֹ אֲשֶׁר בְּשׁוּשַׁן הַבִּירָה:

Esther
CHAPTER 1

4 · אסתר
פרק א

3 in the third year of his reign, he made a banquet for all his nobleman and his servants; the military officials of Persia and Media, the royal family, and the governors of the provinces who were before him.

ג בִּשְׁנַת שָׁלוֹשׁ לְמָלְכוֹ עָשָׂה מִשְׁתֶּה לְכָל־שָׂרָיו וַעֲבָדָיו חֵיל פָּרַס וּמָדַי הַפַּרְתְּמִים וְשָׂרֵי הַמְּדִינוֹת לְפָנָיו:

bish-NAT sha-LOSH l'-mol-KHO a-SAH mish-TEH l'-khol sa-RAV va-a-va-DAV KHAYL pa-RAS u-ma-DAI ha-par-t'-MEEM v'-sa-RAY ha-m'-dee-NOT l'-fa-NAV

4 When he displayed the wealth of his majestic kingdom and the splendorous glory of his grandeur, for many days, one hundred and eighty days.

ד בְּהַרְאֹתוֹ אֶת־עֹשֶׁר כְּבוֹד מַלְכוּתוֹ וְאֶת־יְקָר תִּפְאֶרֶת גְּדוּלָּתוֹ יָמִים רַבִּים שְׁמוֹנִים וּמְאַת יוֹם:

5 When these days were complete, the king made a banquet for all the people that were present in Shushan the capital, for those who were great and small, for seven days, in the court of the garden of the king's palace.

ה וּבִמְלוֹאת הַיָּמִים הָאֵלֶּה עָשָׂה הַמֶּלֶךְ לְכָל־הָעָם הַנִּמְצְאִים בְּשׁוּשַׁן הַבִּירָה לְמִגָּדוֹל וְעַד־קָטָן מִשְׁתֶּה שִׁבְעַת יָמִים בַּחֲצַר גִּנַּת בִּיתַן הַמֶּלֶךְ:

1:3 He made a banquet What reason was there to celebrate in Ahasuerus's third year? The prophet *Yirmiyahu*, who lived at the end of the First Temple period, prophesied that the Children of Israel would be in exile for seventy years (Jeremiah 29:10). According to the Sages (*Megilla* 11b), Ahasuerus erroneously calculated that these seventy years had elapsed, and that *Hashem* had forsaken the Jewish people and the Land of Israel. Not only did he host a celebratory banquet, but the Sages add that he donned the vestments of the High Priest and used captured vessels from the *Beit Hamikdash* to emphasize this point. Punishment was exacted on Queen Vashti, wife of Ahasuerus and the granddaughter of Nebuchadnezzar, the wicked ruler who had destroyed the *Beit Hamikdash*. The Sages teach that Vashti convinced her husband not to allow the rebuilding of the *Beit Hamikdash* in *Yerushalayim* during his reign. Therefore, Vashti is punished.

5 · *Esther*
CHAPTER 1

אסתר
פרק א

6 There were tapestries of white, fine wool, and blue, suspended with cords of fine linen and purple, upon silver rods and pillars of marble. The couches were of gold and silver, upon a floor of alabaster and mosaics of various marble and precious stones.

ו חוּר כַּרְפַּס וּתְכֵלֶת אָחוּז בְּחַבְלֵי־בּוּץ וְאַרְגָּמָן עַל־גְּלִילֵי כֶסֶף וְעַמּוּדֵי שֵׁשׁ מִטּוֹת זָהָב וָכֶסֶף עַל רִצְפַת בַּהַט־וָשֵׁשׁ וְדַר וְסֹחָרֶת:

KHUR kar-PAS ut-KHAY-let a-KHUZ b'-khav-lay VUTZ v'-ar-ga-MAN al g'-LEE-lay KHE-sef v'-a-MU-day SHAYSH mi-TOT za-HAV va-KHE-sef AL ri-tz'-FAT BA-hat va-SHAYSH v'-DAR v'-so-KHA-ret

7 The drinks were served in vessels of gold and the vessels were diverse; the royal wine was in abundance, according to the generosity of the king.

ז וְהַשְׁקוֹת בִּכְלֵי זָהָב וְכֵלִים מִכֵּלִים שׁוֹנִים וְיֵין מַלְכוּת רָב כְּיַד הַמֶּלֶךְ:

8 The drinking was according to the law; no one was coerced, for the king had established for all the officers of his house that they should act according to every man's wish.

ח וְהַשְּׁתִיָּה כַדָּת אֵין אֹנֵס כִּי־כֵן יִסַּד הַמֶּלֶךְ עַל כָּל־רַב בֵּיתוֹ לַעֲשׂוֹת כִּרְצוֹן אִישׁ־וָאִישׁ:

9 Vashti the queen also made a banquet for the women in the royal house of King Ahasuerus.

ט גַּם וַשְׁתִּי הַמַּלְכָּה עָשְׂתָה מִשְׁתֵּה נָשִׁים בֵּית הַמַּלְכוּת אֲשֶׁר לַמֶּלֶךְ אֲחַשְׁוֵרוֹשׁ:

> **1:6 There were tapestries of white, fine wool** The descriptions of the wall hangings in King Ahasuerus's palace are nearly identical to those of the *Mishkan*, Tabernacle (Exodus 36:8). This prompted the *Talmud* (*Megillah* 12a) to understand that upon the exile from Israel after the destruction of the First *Beit Hamikdash*, it's vessels and adornments were taken as booty and became part of the Persian king's treasury. It was precisely these stolen items that were on display at King Ahasuerus's party. Those Jews of Persia who, according to the Sages, refused to join King Ahasuerus's party where these items were displayed, were declaring their loyalty to God and the fallen Temple in *Yerushalayim*.

Esther
CHAPTER 1

10 On the seventh day, when the heart of the king was merry with wine, he commanded Mehuman, Bizzetha, Harbona, Bigtha, Abagtha, Zethar, and Carcas, the seven servants who ministered in the presence of King Ahasuerus,

11 to bring Vashti the queen before the king in the royal crown to display her beauty to the people and the princes, for she was beautiful.

12 Queen Vashti refused to come at the king's command that was brought by the servants. The king became very incensed his anger burned within him.

13 The king then said to the wise men who knew the times, for the king's practice was to turn to all who knew the law and the application of judgment.

14 Those closest to him were Carshena, Shethar, Admatha, Tarshish, Meres, Marsena and Memucan, the seven ministers of Persia and Media, who saw the king's face and were seated first in the kingdom.

15 "What should be done with Queen Vashti according to law for her not fulfilling the order of King Ahasuerus delivered by the servants?"

אסתר · 6
פרק א

י בַּיּוֹם הַשְּׁבִיעִי כְּטוֹב לֵב־הַמֶּלֶךְ בַּיָּיִן אָמַר לִמְהוּמָן בִּזְּתָא חַרְבוֹנָא בִּגְתָא וַאֲבַגְתָא זֵתַר וְכַרְכַּס שִׁבְעַת הַסָּרִיסִים הַמְשָׁרְתִים אֶת־פְּנֵי הַמֶּלֶךְ אֲחַשְׁוֵרוֹשׁ:

יא לְהָבִיא אֶת־וַשְׁתִּי הַמַּלְכָּה לִפְנֵי הַמֶּלֶךְ בְּכֶתֶר מַלְכוּת לְהַרְאוֹת הָעַמִּים וְהַשָּׂרִים אֶת־יָפְיָהּ כִּי־טוֹבַת מַרְאֶה הִיא:

יב וַתְּמָאֵן הַמַּלְכָּה וַשְׁתִּי לָבוֹא בִּדְבַר הַמֶּלֶךְ אֲשֶׁר בְּיַד הַסָּרִיסִים וַיִּקְצֹף הַמֶּלֶךְ מְאֹד וַחֲמָתוֹ בָּעֲרָה בוֹ:

יג וַיֹּאמֶר הַמֶּלֶךְ לַחֲכָמִים יֹדְעֵי הָעִתִּים כִּי־כֵן דְּבַר הַמֶּלֶךְ לִפְנֵי כָּל־יֹדְעֵי דָּת וָדִין:

יד וְהַקָּרֹב אֵלָיו כַּרְשְׁנָא שֵׁתָר אַדְמָתָא תַרְשִׁישׁ מֶרֶס מַרְסְנָא מְמוּכָן שִׁבְעַת שָׂרֵי פָּרַס וּמָדַי רֹאֵי פְּנֵי הַמֶּלֶךְ הַיֹּשְׁבִים רִאשֹׁנָה בַּמַּלְכוּת:

טו כְּדָת מַה־לַּעֲשׂוֹת בַּמַּלְכָּה וַשְׁתִּי עַל אֲשֶׁר לֹא־עָשְׂתָה אֶת־מַאֲמַר הַמֶּלֶךְ אֲחַשְׁוֵרוֹשׁ בְּיַד הַסָּרִיסִים:

Esther
CHAPTER 1

16 Memucan answered before the king and the ministers, "Vashti the queen has not only done wrong to the king, but also to all the ministers and all the people that are in all the provinces of King Ahasuerus.

17 For the matter of the queen will go out to all women to disgrace their husbands in their eyes when it will be recalled that King Ahasuerus commanded Vashti the queen to be brought before him, but she did not come.

18 On that day, the princesses of Persia and Media who have heard about the act of the queen will speak about it to all of the king's ministers causing sufficient disgrace and anger.

19 If it is pleasing to the king, let a royal commandment be sent out from before him, and let it be written among the laws of Persia and Media, which should not be repealed, that Vashti should no longer come before King Ahasuerus, and that the king grant her royal status to another who is worthier than she.

20 When the king's decree which he shall make will be heard throughout all his kingdom, though it is vast, all wives will give honor to their husbands from the greatest to the smallest."

אסתר
פרק א

טז וַיֹּאמֶר מוֹמְכָן [מְמוּכָן] לִפְנֵי הַמֶּלֶךְ וְהַשָּׂרִים לֹא עַל־הַמֶּלֶךְ לְבַדּוֹ עָוְתָה וַשְׁתִּי הַמַּלְכָּה כִּי עַל־כָּל־הַשָּׂרִים וְעַל־כָּל־הָעַמִּים אֲשֶׁר בְּכָל־מְדִינוֹת הַמֶּלֶךְ אֲחַשְׁוֵרוֹשׁ:

יז כִּי־יֵצֵא דְבַר־הַמַּלְכָּה עַל־כָּל־הַנָּשִׁים לְהַבְזוֹת בַּעְלֵיהֶן בְּעֵינֵיהֶן בְּאָמְרָם הַמֶּלֶךְ אֲחַשְׁוֵרוֹשׁ אָמַר לְהָבִיא אֶת־וַשְׁתִּי הַמַּלְכָּה לְפָנָיו וְלֹא־בָאָה:

יח וְהַיּוֹם הַזֶּה תֹּאמַרְנָה שָׂרוֹת פָּרַס־וּמָדַי אֲשֶׁר שָׁמְעוּ אֶת־דְּבַר הַמַּלְכָּה לְכֹל שָׂרֵי הַמֶּלֶךְ וּכְדַי בִּזָּיוֹן וָקָצֶף:

יט אִם־עַל־הַמֶּלֶךְ טוֹב יֵצֵא דְבַר־מַלְכוּת מִלְּפָנָיו וְיִכָּתֵב בְּדָתֵי פָרַס־וּמָדַי וְלֹא יַעֲבוֹר אֲשֶׁר לֹא־תָבוֹא וַשְׁתִּי לִפְנֵי הַמֶּלֶךְ אֲחַשְׁוֵרוֹשׁ וּמַלְכוּתָהּ יִתֵּן הַמֶּלֶךְ לִרְעוּתָהּ הַטּוֹבָה מִמֶּנָּה:

כ וְנִשְׁמַע פִּתְגָם הַמֶּלֶךְ אֲשֶׁר־יַעֲשֶׂה בְּכָל־מַלְכוּתוֹ כִּי רַבָּה הִיא וְכָל־הַנָּשִׁים יִתְּנוּ יְקָר לְבַעְלֵיהֶן לְמִגָּדוֹל וְעַד־קָטָן:

Esther
CHAPTER 1

21 The matter was good in the eyes of the king and the ministers, and the king did in accordance with the advice of Memucan;

22 He sent scrolls to all the king's provinces, to every province according to its own script, and to every people according to its language, stating that every man should rule in his own house, and speak according to the language of his nation.

אסתר · 8
פרק א

כא וַיִּיטַב הַדָּבָר בְּעֵינֵי הַמֶּלֶךְ וְהַשָּׂרִים וַיַּעַשׂ הַמֶּלֶךְ כִּדְבַר מְמוּכָן:

כב וַיִּשְׁלַח סְפָרִים אֶל־כָּל־מְדִינוֹת הַמֶּלֶךְ אֶל־מְדִינָה וּמְדִינָה כִּכְתָבָהּ וְאֶל־עַם וָעָם כִּלְשׁוֹנוֹ לִהְיוֹת כָּל־אִישׁ שֹׂרֵר בְּבֵיתוֹ וּמְדַבֵּר כִּלְשׁוֹן עַמּוֹ:

CHAPTER 2
פרק ב

CHAPTER 2

AFTER AHASUERUS'S ANGER SUBSIDES, HE IS DESPONDENT over what happened with Vashti. His servants suggest he gather women from all of his empire and choose a new wife. There is a Jew living in Shushan named *Mordechai*, who had been exiled from *Yerushalayim* prior to the destruction of the *Beit Hamikdash*. He is raising his cousin, *Hadassah* or *Esther*, since she has no parents. When the women are gathered to the king's palace, *Esther* is also taken. She finds favor in everyone's eyes and is given preferential treatment. However, she does not reveal her lineage as *Mordechai* has instructed her to keep it a secret. *Esther* appears before the king, and he selects her as his new queen. *Mordechai* establishes his presence at the king's gate so he can watch over *Esther* in the palace. While there, he overhears Bigthan and Teresh, two of the king's guards, plotting to assassinate the king. *Mordechai* reveals the plot to *Esther*, who warns Ahasuerus. Bigthan and Teresh are executed, and the matter is recorded in the king's record book.

1 After these events transpired, when the wrath of King Ahasuerus abated, he remembered Vashti and what she had done, as well as what was decreed against her.

א אַחַר הַדְּבָרִים הָאֵלֶּה כְּשֹׁךְ חֲמַת הַמֶּלֶךְ אֲחַשְׁוֵרוֹשׁ זָכַר אֶת־וַשְׁתִּי וְאֵת אֲשֶׁר־עָשָׂתָה וְאֵת אֲשֶׁר־נִגְזַר עָלֶיהָ:

2 The youthful servants of the king suggested, "Let young, attractive virgins be sought out for the king.

ב וַיֹּאמְרוּ נַעֲרֵי־הַמֶּלֶךְ מְשָׁרְתָיו יְבַקְשׁוּ לַמֶּלֶךְ נְעָרוֹת בְּתוּלוֹת טוֹבוֹת מַרְאֶה:

Esther
CHAPTER 2

3 Furthermore, the king should appoint officers in all the provinces of his kingdom so that they may assemble every young, attractive virgin to Shushan the capital, to the harem under the custody of Hege, the king's eunuch, the guardian of the women; and let their cosmetics be given to them.

4 The young woman who finds favor in the eyes of the king will become the queen instead of Vashti." The matter was pleasing in the eyes of the king, and he followed their suggestion.

5 There was a Jewish man in the capital of Shushan, whose name was *Mordechai ben Ya'ir ben Shim'i ben Keesh*, from the tribe of *Binyamin*,

12 · אסתר
פרק ב

ג וַיַּפְקֵד הַמֶּלֶךְ פְּקִידִים בְּכָל־מְדִינוֹת מַלְכוּתוֹ וְיִקְבְּצוּ אֶת־כָּל־נַעֲרָה־בְתוּלָה טוֹבַת מַרְאֶה אֶל־שׁוּשַׁן הַבִּירָה אֶל־בֵּית הַנָּשִׁים אֶל־יַד הֵגֶא סְרִיס הַמֶּלֶךְ שֹׁמֵר הַנָּשִׁים וְנָתוֹן תַּמְרוּקֵיהֶן:

ד וְהַנַּעֲרָה אֲשֶׁר תִּיטַב בְּעֵינֵי הַמֶּלֶךְ תִּמְלֹךְ תַּחַת וַשְׁתִּי וַיִּיטַב הַדָּבָר בְּעֵינֵי הַמֶּלֶךְ וַיַּעַשׂ כֵּן:

ה אִישׁ יְהוּדִי הָיָה בְּשׁוּשַׁן הַבִּירָה וּשְׁמוֹ מָרְדֳּכַי בֶּן יָאִיר בֶּן־שִׁמְעִי בֶּן־קִישׁ אִישׁ יְמִינִי:

EESH y'-hu-DEE ha-YAH b'-shu-SHAN ha-bee-RAH ush-MO mor-d'-KHAI BEN ya-EER ben shim-EE ben KEESH EESH y'-mee-NEE

2:5 From the tribe of *Binyamin*
Mordechai, from the tribe *Binyamin*, was a descendant of King *Shaul*. When *Shaul* was commanded to obliterate the nation of Amalek, he felt this command was too cruel and spared Agag, their king. This error ultimately led to the birth of Haman. In *Megillat Esther*, *Mordechai* and *Esther* rectify the sin of their ancestor by defeating Haman and overcoming the descendants of Amalek. Furthermore, instead of having mercy on *Esther* who had reservations about approaching King Ahasuerus unbidden, *Mordechai* told her to go despite the danger involved. What appeared cruel, resulted in the salvation of the Jewish people. In the modern State of Israel, leadership must balance proper compassion for combatants with the duty of keeping Israel safe. We learn from *Shaul*'s misplaced mercy that a failure to do so can have disastrous consequences down the line.

13 • *Esther*
CHAPTER 2

אסתר
פרק ב

6 who had been exiled from *Yerushalayim* along with those exiled with *Yechonya*, the King of *Yehuda*, who Nebuchadnezzar, the King of Babylonia, expelled.

ו אֲשֶׁר הָגְלָה מִירוּשָׁלַיִם עִם־הַגֹּלָה אֲשֶׁר הָגְלְתָה עִם יְכָנְיָה מֶלֶךְ־יְהוּדָה אֲשֶׁר הֶגְלָה נְבוּכַדְנֶאצַּר מֶלֶךְ בָּבֶל׃

a-SHER hog-LAH mee-ru-sha-LA-yim im ha-go-LAH a-SHER hog-l'-TAH IM y'-khon-YAH ME-lekh y'-hu-DAH a-SHER heg-LAH n'-vu-khad-ne-TZAR ME-lekh ba-VEL

7 He had raised *Hadassah*, that is, *Esther*, his uncle's daughter; for she had no father or mother. The young woman was beautiful and attractive. When her father and mother died, *Mordechai* took her in as a daughter.

ז וַיְהִי אֹמֵן אֶת־הֲדַסָּה הִיא אֶסְתֵּר בַּת־דֹּדוֹ כִּי אֵין לָהּ אָב וָאֵם וְהַנַּעֲרָה יְפַת־תֹּאַר וְטוֹבַת מַרְאֶה וּבְמוֹת אָבִיהָ וְאִמָּהּ לְקָחָהּ מָרְדֳּכַי לוֹ לְבַת׃

8 And it was that when the proclamation of the king and his order to gather abundant young women to the capital of Shushan under the supervision of Hegai, *Esther* was taken into the king's harem, to the custody of Hegai, guardian of the women.

ח וַיְהִי בְּהִשָּׁמַע דְּבַר־הַמֶּלֶךְ וְדָתוֹ וּבְהִקָּבֵץ נְעָרוֹת רַבּוֹת אֶל־שׁוּשַׁן הַבִּירָה אֶל־יַד הֵגָי וַתִּלָּקַח אֶסְתֵּר אֶל־בֵּית הַמֶּלֶךְ אֶל־יַד הֵגַי שֹׁמֵר הַנָּשִׁים׃

9 The young woman found favor in his eyes and she benefited from his kindness. He was quick to give her cosmetics and portions of food, as well as seven maidens who were provided to her from the king's palace. He enhanced treatment of her and her servants in the harem.

ט וַתִּיטַב הַנַּעֲרָה בְעֵינָיו וַתִּשָּׂא חֶסֶד לְפָנָיו וַיְבַהֵל אֶת־תַּמְרוּקֶיהָ וְאֶת־מָנוֹתֶהָ לָתֵת לָהּ וְאֵת שֶׁבַע הַנְּעָרוֹת הָרְאֻיוֹת לָתֶת־לָהּ מִבֵּית הַמֶּלֶךְ וַיְשַׁנֶּהָ וְאֶת־נַעֲרוֹתֶיהָ לְטוֹב בֵּית הַנָּשִׁים׃

2:6 Exiled from Yerushalayim The Hebrew word for exile is golah (גולה), while the term for 'redemption' is geulah (גאולה). The words are similar, and the only difference between the two words is the Hebrew letter aleph (א). The numerical value of the aleph is one, representing the one true God. This reminds us that

Esther
CHAPTER 2

10 *Esther* did not reveal her nation or heritage since *Mordechai* commanded her not to disclose it.

11 *Mordechai* walked every day before the court of the harem to know *Esther*'s wellbeing and what would become of her.

12 Now, when it was the turn of every young woman to come to King Ahasuerus at the conclusion of the twelve months of preparation decreed for each woman, for in this way they completed their cosmetic treatment – six months with oil of myrrh and six months with perfumes and women's cosmetics.

13 With this each woman would come before the king. Whatever she requested was given to her to bring with her from the harem to the king's palace.

14 In the evening she arrived and in the morning she returned to the second harem, to the custody of Sha'ashgaz, the king's eunuch, who guarded the concubines. Each woman no longer came to the king unless the king desired her and she was called by name.

14 · אסתר
פרק ב

י לֹא־הִגִּ֣ידָה אֶסְתֵּ֔ר אֶת־עַמָּ֖הּ וְאֶת־מֽוֹלַדְתָּ֑הּ כִּ֧י מָרְדֳּכַ֛י צִוָּ֥ה עָלֶ֖יהָ אֲשֶׁ֥ר לֹא־תַגִּֽיד׃

יא וּבְכָל־י֣וֹם וָי֔וֹם מָרְדֳּכַי֙ מִתְהַלֵּ֔ךְ לִפְנֵ֖י חֲצַ֣ר בֵּית־הַנָּשִׁ֑ים לָדַ֙עַת֙ אֶת־שְׁל֣וֹם אֶסְתֵּ֔ר וּמַה־יֵּעָשֶׂ֖ה בָּֽהּ׃

יב וּבְהַגִּ֡יעַ תֹּר֩ נַעֲרָ֨ה וְנַעֲרָ֜ה לָב֣וֹא ׀ אֶל־הַמֶּ֣לֶךְ אֲחַשְׁוֵר֗וֹשׁ מִקֵּץ֩ הֱי֨וֹת לָ֜הּ כְּדָ֤ת הַנָּשִׁים֙ שְׁנֵ֣ים עָשָׂ֣ר חֹ֔דֶשׁ כִּ֛י כֵּ֥ן יִמְלְא֖וּ יְמֵ֣י מְרוּקֵיהֶ֑ן שִׁשָּׁ֤ה חֳדָשִׁים֙ בְּשֶׁ֣מֶן הַמֹּ֔ר וְשִׁשָּׁ֤ה חֳדָשִׁים֙ בַּבְּשָׂמִ֔ים וּבְתַמְרוּקֵ֖י הַנָּשִֽׁים׃

יג וּבָזֶ֕ה הַֽנַּעֲרָ֖ה בָּאָ֣ה אֶל־הַמֶּ֑לֶךְ אֵת֩ כׇּל־אֲשֶׁ֨ר תֹּאמַ֜ר יִנָּ֤תֵֽן לָהּ֙ לָב֣וֹא עִמָּ֔הּ מִבֵּ֥ית הַנָּשִׁ֖ים עַד־בֵּ֥ית הַמֶּֽלֶךְ׃

יד בָּעֶ֣רֶב ׀ הִ֣יא בָאָ֗ה וּ֠בַבֹּ֠קֶר הִ֣יא שָׁבָ֞ה אֶל־בֵּ֤ית הַנָּשִׁים֙ שֵׁנִ֔י אֶל־יַ֧ד שַֽׁעַשְׁגַ֛ז סְרִ֥יס הַמֶּ֖לֶךְ שֹׁמֵ֣ר הַפִּֽילַגְשִׁ֑ים לֹא־תָב֥וֹא עוֹד֙ אֶל־הַמֶּ֔לֶךְ כִּ֣י אִם־חָפֵ֥ץ בָּ֛הּ הַמֶּ֖לֶךְ וְנִקְרְאָ֥ה בְשֵֽׁם׃

> to go from exile to redemption we must focus our hearts on the one true God. We must ask ourselves how we can best follow Him and where we can best serve Him in order to turn the golah (exile) into the geulah (redemption).

15 · *Esther*
CHAPTER 2

15 When the time for *Esther bat Avichayil*, the uncle of *Mordechai*, who had taken her for his daughter, arrived to go to the king, she requested nothing except for that which Hegai the king's eunuch, the keeper of the women recommended. *Esther* found favor in the eyes of all who saw her.

16 *Esther* was taken to King Ahasuerus, into his royal palace, in the tenth month, which is the month *Tevet*, in the seventh year of his reign.

17 The king loved *Esther* more than the other women, and she attained his grace and favor more than all the virgins; so that he placed the royal crown upon her head and made her queen instead of Vashti.

18 Then the king made a great banquet for all his ministers and his servants known as the banquet of *Esther*. He lowered taxes for his provinces and disseminated gifts according to his royal ability.

19 When the virgins were gathered together a second time, *Mordechai* sat in the king's gate.

20 *Esther* had not yet made known her ancestry or her nationality as *Mordechai* had directed her. That which *Mordechai* told her she did, just as when she was raised by him.

אסתר
פרק ב

טו וּבְהַגִּיעַ תֹּר־אֶסְתֵּר בַּת־אֲבִיחַיִל דֹּד מָרְדֳּכַי אֲשֶׁר לָקַח־לוֹ לְבַת לָבוֹא אֶל־הַמֶּלֶךְ לֹא בִקְשָׁה דָּבָר כִּי אִם אֶת־אֲשֶׁר יֹאמַר הֵגַי סְרִיס־הַמֶּלֶךְ שֹׁמֵר הַנָּשִׁים וַתְּהִי אֶסְתֵּר נֹשֵׂאת חֵן בְּעֵינֵי כָּל־רֹאֶיהָ:

טז וַתִּלָּקַח אֶסְתֵּר אֶל־הַמֶּלֶךְ אֲחַשְׁוֵרוֹשׁ אֶל־בֵּית מַלְכוּתוֹ בַּחֹדֶשׁ הָעֲשִׂירִי הוּא־חֹדֶשׁ טֵבֵת בִּשְׁנַת־שֶׁבַע לְמַלְכוּתוֹ:

יז וַיֶּאֱהַב הַמֶּלֶךְ אֶת־אֶסְתֵּר מִכָּל־הַנָּשִׁים וַתִּשָּׂא־חֵן וָחֶסֶד לְפָנָיו מִכָּל־הַבְּתוּלֹת וַיָּשֶׂם כֶּתֶר־מַלְכוּת בְּרֹאשָׁהּ וַיַּמְלִיכֶהָ תַּחַת וַשְׁתִּי:

יח וַיַּעַשׂ הַמֶּלֶךְ מִשְׁתֶּה גָדוֹל לְכָל־שָׂרָיו וַעֲבָדָיו אֵת מִשְׁתֵּה אֶסְתֵּר וַהֲנָחָה לַמְּדִינוֹת עָשָׂה וַיִּתֵּן מַשְׂאֵת כְּיַד הַמֶּלֶךְ:

יט וּבְהִקָּבֵץ בְּתוּלוֹת שֵׁנִית וּמָרְדֳּכַי יֹשֵׁב בְּשַׁעַר־הַמֶּלֶךְ:

כ אֵין אֶסְתֵּר מַגֶּדֶת מוֹלַדְתָּהּ וְאֶת־עַמָּהּ כַּאֲשֶׁר צִוָּה עָלֶיהָ מָרְדֳּכָי וְאֶת־מַאֲמַר מָרְדֳּכַי אֶסְתֵּר עֹשָׂה כַּאֲשֶׁר הָיְתָה בְאָמְנָה אִתּוֹ:

Esther
CHAPTER 2

21 In those days, while *Mordechai* sat in the king's gate, two of the king's eunuchs, Bigthan and Teresh, guardians of the entrance to the king's inner chamber, were infuriated, and sought to raise their hand against King Ahasuerus.

22 The matter became known to *Mordechai*, who told it to Queen *Esther,* and *Esther* reported it to the king in *Mordechai*'s name.

> va-yi-va-DA ha-da-VAR l'-mor-d'-KHAI va-ya-GAYD l'-es-TAYR ha-mal-KAH va-TO-mer es-TAYR la-ME-lekh b'-SHAYM mor-d'-KHAI

23 An investigation was conducted and revealed. They were both hanged on gallows, and it was written in the annals before the king.

16 • אסתר
פרק ב

כא בַּיָּמִים הָהֵם וּמָרְדֳּכַי יֹשֵׁב בְּשַׁעַר־הַמֶּלֶךְ קָצַף בִּגְתָן וָתֶרֶשׁ שְׁנֵי־סָרִיסֵי הַמֶּלֶךְ מִשֹּׁמְרֵי הַסַּף וַיְבַקְשׁוּ לִשְׁלֹחַ יָד בַּמֶּלֶךְ אֲחַשְׁוֵרֹשׁ:

כב וַיִּוָּדַע הַדָּבָר לְמָרְדֳּכַי וַיַּגֵּד לְאֶסְתֵּר הַמַּלְכָּה וַתֹּאמֶר אֶסְתֵּר לַמֶּלֶךְ בְּשֵׁם מָרְדֳּכָי:

כג וַיְבֻקַּשׁ הַדָּבָר וַיִּמָּצֵא וַיִּתָּלוּ שְׁנֵיהֶם עַל־עֵץ וַיִּכָּתֵב בְּסֵפֶר דִּבְרֵי הַיָּמִים לִפְנֵי הַמֶּלֶךְ:

2:22 Known to *Mordechai* How did *Mordechai* learn what these two royal guards were plotting? According to Jewish tradition, *Mordechai* was a great scholar who understood seventy different languages and was therefore able to decipher their conversation. Knowing additional languages helped *Mordechai* bring salvation to the Jews of Shushan. The prophets describe how in the future, language will become even more important as the whole world will learn to speak Hebrew. *Tzefanya* (3:9) promises that, "I will change the nations and grant them purity of speech, so they will all call out in the name of *Hashem* and serve Him with one accord." Just like God used language to trigger a pivotal turning point in the *Megillah,* in the end of days, learning the holy language of Hebrew will bring an epic change to the world as well.

CHAPTER 3
פרק ג

CHAPTER 3

FIVE YEARS LATER, AHASUERUS APPOINTS A NEW VICEROY named Haman. He decrees that all of his subjects must bow before Haman, which they do with the exception of *Mordechai*. When Haman finds out that *Mordechai* will not bow down to him, he becomes furious and determines to take revenge on the entire Jewish people. Haman draws lots to determine on which date to execute his plan, and the 13th day of the month of *Adar* is selected. Appearing before Ahasuerus, Haman describes the Jewish people as a scattered nation that does not keep the king's laws. He promises 10,000 silver talents if the king will let him destroy the Jews. Ahasuerus refuses the payment, but gives Haman his signet ring to do with it as he wishes. Haman sends messengers throughout the kingdom with the decree to annihilate the Jews on the 13th of *Adar*. Ahasuerus and Haman sit down to celebrate, and the Jews of Shushan are confused.

1 After these events transpired, King Ahasuerus promoted Haman, the son of Hammedatha the Agagite and raised his stature. He placed his governmental position above the other ministers who were with him.

א אַחַר הַדְּבָרִים הָאֵלֶּה גִּדַּל הַמֶּלֶךְ אֲחַשְׁוֵרוֹשׁ אֶת־הָמָן בֶּן־הַמְּדָתָא הָאֲגָגִי וַיְנַשְּׂאֵהוּ וַיָּשֶׂם אֶת־כִּסְאוֹ מֵעַל כָּל־הַשָּׂרִים אֲשֶׁר אִתּוֹ:

3:1 Haman the son of Hammedatha the Agagite The Sages teach that Haman was referred to as an Agagite because he descended from the Amalekite king Agag. When King *Shaul* was instructed to eradicate the evil Amalekites, he fell short of fulfilling *Hashem*'s command when he kept alive their king and some of their animals (1 Samuel 15). Amalek represents the epitome of evil, as they sought to destroy the People of Israel following the Exodus from Egypt for no particular reason. Therefore, *Hashem* commands the Children of Israel to wipe out this tribe of evil doers (Exodus 17:14–16 and Deuteronomy 25:19). Throughout history,

Esther
CHAPTER 3

a-KHAR ha-d'-va-REEM ha-AY-leh gi-DAL ha-ME-lekh a-khash-vay-ROSH et ha-MAN BEN ha-m'-DA-ta ha-a-ga-GEE vai-na-s'-AY-hu va-YA-sem et kis-O may-AL kol ha-sa-REEM a-SHER i-TO

2 All of the servants of the king who were in the king's court bowed and prostrated themselves before Haman since they were commanded to do so by the king. However, *Mordechai* would not bow or prostrate himself.

3 The servants of the king who were in the king's courtyard said to *Mordechai*, "Why do you violate the decree of the king?"

4 And it was that when they would say this to him every day, he would not listen to them. They told Haman in order to see whether *Mordechai* would remain firm in his objection since he told them that he was a Jew.

5 Haman saw that *Mordechai* did not bow or prostrate himself, and he became full of fury.

6 Haman spurned the idea of killing only *Mordechai* since they related to him *Mordechai*'s nationality. Haman, rather, sought to annihilate all the Jews in the kingdom of Ahasuerus since they were from the nation of *Mordechai*.

ב וְכָל־עַבְדֵי הַמֶּלֶךְ אֲשֶׁר־בְּשַׁעַר הַמֶּלֶךְ כֹּרְעִים וּמִשְׁתַּחֲוִים לְהָמָן כִּי־כֵן צִוָּה־לוֹ הַמֶּלֶךְ וּמָרְדֳּכַי לֹא יִכְרַע וְלֹא יִשְׁתַּחֲוֶה:

ג וַיֹּאמְרוּ עַבְדֵי הַמֶּלֶךְ אֲשֶׁר־בְּשַׁעַר הַמֶּלֶךְ לְמָרְדֳּכָי מַדּוּעַ אַתָּה עוֹבֵר אֵת מִצְוַת הַמֶּלֶךְ:

ד וַיְהִי באמרם [כְּאָמְרָם] אֵלָיו יוֹם וָיוֹם וְלֹא שָׁמַע אֲלֵיהֶם וַיַּגִּידוּ לְהָמָן לִרְאוֹת הֲיַעַמְדוּ דִּבְרֵי מָרְדֳּכַי כִּי־הִגִּיד לָהֶם אֲשֶׁר־הוּא יְהוּדִי:

ה וַיַּרְא הָמָן כִּי־אֵין מָרְדֳּכַי כֹּרֵעַ וּמִשְׁתַּחֲוֶה לוֹ וַיִּמָּלֵא הָמָן חֵמָה:

ו וַיִּבֶז בְּעֵינָיו לִשְׁלֹחַ יָד בְּמָרְדֳּכַי לְבַדּוֹ כִּי־הִגִּידוּ לוֹ אֶת־עַם מָרְדֳּכָי וַיְבַקֵּשׁ הָמָן לְהַשְׁמִיד אֶת־כָּל־הַיְּהוּדִים אֲשֶׁר בְּכָל־מַלְכוּת אֲחַשְׁוֵרוֹשׁ עַם מָרְדֳּכָי:

there have been continual battles with Amalek such as the one described in *Megillat Esther*. Often it looks like Amalek or their successors might be victorious. However, in the end God's people will always succeed. This is one of the great lessons of Jewish history. Though it may take many years, the Jewish People will always overcome their enemies.

Esther
CHAPTER 3

7 In the first month, which is the Month of *Nisan*, in the twelfth year since Ahasuerus became the king, a *pur*, which is a lot, was cast before Haman to calculate every day and month. It fell out on the twelfth month, which is the month of *Adar*.

8 Haman said to King Ahasuerus, "There is one nation that is scattered and separated among the nations in all the provinces of your kingdom, and their laws are different from those of every nation. They do not uphold the laws of the king, and there is no benefit to the king to let them live.

9 If it pleases the king, he should issue a proclamation to have them annihilated and I will pay ten-thousand talents of silver to the royal laborers to bring to the treasury."

אסתר
פרק ג

ז בַּחֹדֶשׁ הָרִאשׁוֹן הוּא־חֹדֶשׁ נִיסָן בִּשְׁנַת שְׁתֵּים עֶשְׂרֵה לַמֶּלֶךְ אֲחַשְׁוֵרוֹשׁ הִפִּיל פּוּר הוּא הַגּוֹרָל לִפְנֵי הָמָן מִיּוֹם לְיוֹם וּמֵחֹדֶשׁ לְחֹדֶשׁ שְׁנֵים־עָשָׂר הוּא־חֹדֶשׁ אֲדָר:

ח וַיֹּאמֶר הָמָן לַמֶּלֶךְ אֲחַשְׁוֵרוֹשׁ יֶשְׁנוֹ עַם־אֶחָד מְפֻזָּר וּמְפֹרָד בֵּין הָעַמִּים בְּכֹל מְדִינוֹת מַלְכוּתֶךָ וְדָתֵיהֶם שֹׁנוֹת מִכָּל־עָם וְאֶת־דָּתֵי הַמֶּלֶךְ אֵינָם עֹשִׂים וְלַמֶּלֶךְ אֵין־שֹׁוֶה לְהַנִּיחָם:

ט אִם־עַל־הַמֶּלֶךְ טוֹב יִכָּתֵב לְאַבְּדָם וַעֲשֶׂרֶת אֲלָפִים כִּכַּר־כֶּסֶף אֶשְׁקוֹל עַל־יְדֵי עֹשֵׂי הַמְּלָאכָה לְהָבִיא אֶל־גִּנְזֵי הַמֶּלֶךְ:

im al ha-ME-lekh TOV yi-ka-TAYV l'-a-b'-DAM va-a-SE-ret a-la-FEEM ki-kar KE-sef esh-KOL al y'-DAY o-SAY ha-m'-la-KHAH l'-ha-VEE el gin-ZAY ha-ME-lekh

3:9 I will pay ten-thousand talents of silver The Hebrew word for silver is *kesef* (כסף), related to the verb *kasaf* (כ-ס-ף) which means, to yearn. Money is something for which all people yearn, and that is what gives it its value. Here, Haman hopes that Ahasuerus's desire for wealth will persuade him to agree to wipe out the Jewish people. One way to correct Haman and Ahasuerus's inappropriate yearning for money, is to elevate it for holy and worthwhile purposes. This is why the verse later on, in 9:22, describes the appropriate way to celebrate the holiday of *Purim* as "an occasion of sending gifts to one another and presents to the poor." When we give charity, we demonstrate that we don't merely yearn for gold and silver for its own sake, we value money so that we can help other people, especially the poor and needy.

Esther
CHAPTER 3

10 The king then removed the signet ring from his hand and gave it to Haman, the son of Hammedatha the Agagite, the enemy of the Jews.

11 The king said to Haman, "the silver is yours and you may do with this nation as you see fit."

12 The scribes of the king were called on the thirteenth day of the first month and recorded all that Haman decreed for the regional leaders and provincial governors appointed by the king over every province. The decree was written according to the script of every nation and its language. It was written in the name of King Ahasuerus and stamped with the signet ring of the king.

13 The scrolls were then sent with couriers to all the provinces of the king to destroy, kill, and eradicate the Jews, from young to old, children and women, on a single day, on the thirteenth of the twelfth month, the month of *Adar*, and to plunder their spoils.

22 · אסתר
פרק ג

י וַיָּסַר הַמֶּלֶךְ אֶת־טַבַּעְתּוֹ מֵעַל יָדוֹ וַיִּתְּנָהּ לְהָמָן בֶּן־הַמְּדָתָא הָאֲגָגִי צֹרֵר הַיְּהוּדִים:

יא וַיֹּאמֶר הַמֶּלֶךְ לְהָמָן הַכֶּסֶף נָתוּן לָךְ וְהָעָם לַעֲשׂוֹת בּוֹ כַּטּוֹב בְּעֵינֶיךָ:

יב וַיִּקָּרְאוּ סֹפְרֵי הַמֶּלֶךְ בַּחֹדֶשׁ הָרִאשׁוֹן בִּשְׁלוֹשָׁה עָשָׂר יוֹם בּוֹ וַיִּכָּתֵב כְּכָל־אֲשֶׁר־צִוָּה הָמָן אֶל אֲחַשְׁדַּרְפְּנֵי־הַמֶּלֶךְ וְאֶל־הַפַּחוֹת אֲשֶׁר ׀ עַל־מְדִינָה וּמְדִינָה וְאֶל־שָׂרֵי עַם וָעָם מְדִינָה וּמְדִינָה כִּכְתָבָהּ וְעַם וָעָם כִּלְשׁוֹנוֹ בְּשֵׁם הַמֶּלֶךְ אֲחַשְׁוֵרֹשׁ נִכְתָּב וְנֶחְתָּם בְּטַבַּעַת הַמֶּלֶךְ:

יג וְנִשְׁלוֹחַ סְפָרִים בְּיַד הָרָצִים אֶל־כָּל־מְדִינוֹת הַמֶּלֶךְ לְהַשְׁמִיד לַהֲרֹג וּלְאַבֵּד אֶת־כָּל־הַיְּהוּדִים מִנַּעַר וְעַד־זָקֵן טַף וְנָשִׁים בְּיוֹם אֶחָד בִּשְׁלוֹשָׁה עָשָׂר לְחֹדֶשׁ שְׁנֵים־עָשָׂר הוּא־חֹדֶשׁ אֲדָר וּשְׁלָלָם לָבוֹז:

v'-nish-LO-akh s'-fa-REEM b'-YAD ha-ra-TZEEM el kol m'-dee-NOT ha-ME-lekh l'-hash-MEED la-ha-ROG ul-a-BAYD et kol ha-y'-hu-DEEM mi-NA-ar v'-AD za-KAYN taf v'-na-SHEEM b'-YOM e-KHAD bish-lo-SHAH a-SAR l'-KHO-desh sh'-NAYM a-SAR hu KHO-desh a-DAR ush-la-LAM la-VOZ

3:13 To destroy, kill, and eradicate the Jews Usually, the *Torah* provides the reason why an individual, or the Jewish nation as a whole, is punished. *Megillat Esther*, however, does not explicitly state what the people did to deserve

23 · *Esther*
CHAPTER 3

אסתר
פרק ג

14 The text of the document was to establish the law in every single province. It was to be known to all the people so that they would be prepared for that day.

יד פַּתְשֶׁגֶן הַכְּתָב לְהִנָּתֵן דָּת בְּכָל־מְדִינָה וּמְדִינָה גָּלוּי לְכָל־הָעַמִּים לִהְיוֹת עֲתִדִים לַיּוֹם הַזֶּה:

pat-SHE-gen ha-k'-TAV l'-hi-NA-tayn DAT b'-khol m'-dee-NAH um-dee-NAH ga-LUY l'-khol ha-a-MEEM lih-YOT a-ti-DEEM la-YOM ha-ZEH

the threat of annihilation. When viewed in historical context, it becomes clear that the Jews of Shushan were guilty for not having returned to *Eretz Yisrael* even though they had the opportunity to do so. After the Persian king Cyrus conquered the Babylonians, he allowed the Children of Israel to return to the Land of Israel and begin reconstruction of the *Beit Hamikdash*. However, a mere 42,360 returned to *Yerushalayim* (Ezra 2:64) while close to a million remained in Babylonia. The generation was therefore punished for their lack of enthusiasm towards returning to Israel. This teaches us the importance of making every effort to embrace the land and to physically return to it whenever possible.

3:14 Prepared for that day Many times in history, the enemies of the Jewish people eagerly awaited the day when the Jews would finally meet their ultimate demise. Alas, their plans have always been divinely foiled. In the spring of 1967, Israel's fate seemed truly doomed as nearly all of her neighbors sought to wipe her off the map. Abba Eban, serving at that time as Israel's Foreign Minister, described the mood in the days leading up to the Six Day War: "There was no doubt that the howling mobs in Cairo, Damascus and Baghdad were seeing savage visions of murder and booty. Israel, for its part, had learned from Jewish history that no outrage against its men, women and children, was inconceivable. Many things in Jewish history are too terrible to be believed, but nothing in that history is too terrible to have happened. Memories of the European slaughter were taking form and substance in countless Israeli hearts. They flowed into our room like turgid air and sat heavy on all our minds. As has always been the case, God had different plans, and the young State of Israel mightily and miraculously defeated its enemies."

Esther
CHAPTER 3

15 The couriers went out speedily at the command of the king, and the decree was shared in the capital of Shushan. The king and Haman then sat down to drink, and the city of Shushan was dumbfounded.

24 · אסתר
פרק ג

טו הָרָצִים יָצְאוּ דְחוּפִים בִּדְבַר הַמֶּלֶךְ וְהַדָּת נִתְּנָה בְּשׁוּשַׁן הַבִּירָה וְהַמֶּלֶךְ וְהָמָן יָשְׁבוּ לִשְׁתּוֹת וְהָעִיר שׁוּשָׁן נָבוֹכָה׃

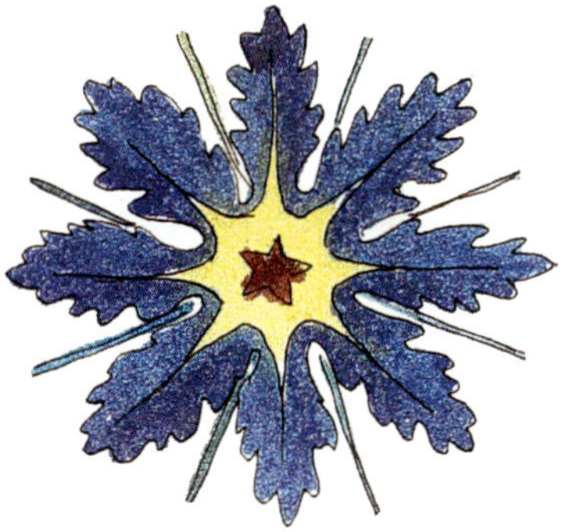

CHAPTER 4
פרק ד

CHAPTER 4

WHEN *MORDECHAI* DISCOVERS HAMAN'S PLOT, HE RENDS his clothing and dons sackcloth and ashes. Wherever news of the decree reaches, the Jews react similarly. Through messengers, *Mordechai* tells *Esther* the content of Haman's decree. He instructs her to appear before the king and plead for the life of her people. *Esther* is reluctant to go to the king and replies that it is well known that anyone who appears before the king unbidden is killed, unless the king extends his scepter. *Mordechai* retorts that *Esther* shouldn't think she will be saved because she resides in the king's palace. If she refuses to go, *Hashem* will save the Jewish people regardless, and she will perish. He adds that perhaps this is the very reason why she became queen in the first place. *Esther* agrees, but requests that the Jewish people gather and fast for three days, after which she will appear before the king.

1. And *Mordechai* was aware of all that transpired. Therefore, *Mordechai* tore his clothes and donned sackcloth and ashes. He went through the city and wailed a loud and bitter cry.

א וּמָרְדֳּכַי יָדַע אֶת־כָּל־אֲשֶׁר נַעֲשָׂה וַיִּקְרַע מָרְדֳּכַי אֶת־בְּגָדָיו וַיִּלְבַּשׁ שַׂק וָאֵפֶר וַיֵּצֵא בְּתוֹךְ הָעִיר וַיִּזְעַק זְעָקָה גְדֹלָה וּמָרָה:

2. He came until the gate of the palace since one may not enter the palace gate while wearing sackcloth.

ב וַיָּבוֹא עַד לִפְנֵי שַׁעַר־הַמֶּלֶךְ כִּי אֵין לָבוֹא אֶל־שַׁעַר הַמֶּלֶךְ בִּלְבוּשׁ שָׂק:

3. In every province that the king's proclamation and decree reached, there was great mourning among the Jews, with fasting and crying and dirges; sackcloth and ashes were upon the multitudes.

ג וּבְכָל־מְדִינָה וּמְדִינָה מְקוֹם אֲשֶׁר דְּבַר־הַמֶּלֶךְ וְדָתוֹ מַגִּיעַ אֵבֶל גָּדוֹל לַיְּהוּדִים וְצוֹם וּבְכִי וּמִסְפֵּד שַׂק וָאֵפֶר יֻצַּע לָרַבִּים:

Esther
CHAPTER 4

4 When *Esther*'s maidservants and eunuchs came and informed her, the queen was greatly disturbed. She sent clothing for *Mordechai* to wear in order for him to remove his sackcloth, but he refused to accept them.

5 *Esther* consequently called upon Hathach, one of the eunuchs whom the king had provided for her, and commanded him to go to *Mordechai* to discern what this is and why this is.

6 Hathach went out to *Mordechai* in the city street in front of the palace gate;

7 And *Mordechai* told him all that occurred to him and about the money that Haman had proposed to be reckoned to the treasury for the eradication of the Jews.

8 He also gave him the text of the decree that had been issued in Shushan regarding their destruction so that he should show it to *Esther* and tell her about it, as well as to command her to go to the king and entreat him and plead before him on behalf of her people.

9 Hathach returned and told *Esther* what *Mordechai*'s had said.

10 *Esther* then told Hathach to direct *Mordechai* as follows:

28 • אסתר
פרק ד

ד וַתָּבוֹאינָה נַעֲרוֹת אֶסְתֵּר וְסָרִיסֶיהָ וַיַּגִּידוּ לָהּ וַתִּתְחַלְחַל הַמַּלְכָּה מְאֹד וַתִּשְׁלַח בְּגָדִים לְהַלְבִּישׁ אֶת־מָרְדֳּכַי וּלְהָסִיר שַׂקּוֹ מֵעָלָיו וְלֹא קִבֵּל:

ה וַתִּקְרָא אֶסְתֵּר לַהֲתָךְ מִסָּרִיסֵי הַמֶּלֶךְ אֲשֶׁר הֶעֱמִיד לְפָנֶיהָ וַתְּצַוֵּהוּ עַל־מָרְדֳּכָי לָדַעַת מַה־זֶּה וְעַל־מַה־זֶּה:

ו וַיֵּצֵא הֲתָךְ אֶל־מָרְדֳּכָי אֶל־רְחוֹב הָעִיר אֲשֶׁר לִפְנֵי שַׁעַר־הַמֶּלֶךְ:

ז וַיַּגֶּד־לוֹ מָרְדֳּכַי אֵת כָּל־אֲשֶׁר קָרָהוּ וְאֵת פָּרָשַׁת הַכֶּסֶף אֲשֶׁר אָמַר הָמָן לִשְׁקוֹל עַל־גִּנְזֵי הַמֶּלֶךְ ביהודיים [בַּיְּהוּדִים] לְאַבְּדָם:

ח וְאֶת־פַּתְשֶׁגֶן כְּתָב־הַדָּת אֲשֶׁר־נִתַּן בְּשׁוּשָׁן לְהַשְׁמִידָם נָתַן לוֹ לְהַרְאוֹת אֶת־אֶסְתֵּר וּלְהַגִּיד לָהּ וּלְצַוּוֹת עָלֶיהָ לָבוֹא אֶל־הַמֶּלֶךְ לְהִתְחַנֶּן־לוֹ וּלְבַקֵּשׁ מִלְּפָנָיו עַל־עַמָּהּ:

ט וַיָּבוֹא הֲתָךְ וַיַּגֵּד לְאֶסְתֵּר אֵת דִּבְרֵי מָרְדֳּכָי:

י וַתֹּאמֶר אֶסְתֵּר לַהֲתָךְ וַתְּצַוֵּהוּ אֶל־מָרְדֳּכָי:

29 · Esther
CHAPTER 4

אסתר
פרק ד

11 "All the king's servants and the people of the king's provinces know that if any person, man or woman, comes to the king in the inner chamber without having been summoned, there is but one law for him, which is that he should be executed. He may only live if the king extends the golden scepter to him. And I have not been summoned to come before the king for the last thirty days."

יא כָּל־עַבְדֵי הַמֶּלֶךְ וְעַם־מְדִינוֹת הַמֶּלֶךְ יוֹדְעִים אֲשֶׁר כָּל־אִישׁ וְאִשָּׁה אֲשֶׁר יָבוֹא־אֶל־הַמֶּלֶךְ אֶל־הֶחָצֵר הַפְּנִימִית אֲשֶׁר לֹא־יִקָּרֵא אַחַת דָּתוֹ לְהָמִית לְבַד מֵאֲשֶׁר יוֹשִׁיט־לוֹ הַמֶּלֶךְ אֶת־שַׁרְבִיט הַזָּהָב וְחָיָה וַאֲנִי לֹא נִקְרֵאתִי לָבוֹא אֶל־הַמֶּלֶךְ זֶה שְׁלוֹשִׁים יוֹם:

12 When *Esther*'s message was related to *Mordechai*,

יב וַיַּגִּידוּ לְמָרְדֳּכָי אֵת דִּבְרֵי אֶסְתֵּר:

13 *Mordechai* responded that he should tell *Esther*, "Do not fool yourself that you will escape in the palace, from all the other Jews.

יג וַיֹּאמֶר מָרְדֳּכַי לְהָשִׁיב אֶל־אֶסְתֵּר אַל־תְּדַמִּי בְנַפְשֵׁךְ לְהִמָּלֵט בֵּית־הַמֶּלֶךְ מִכָּל־הַיְּהוּדִים:

14 For if you remain silent at such a time as this, relief and deliverance will come to the Jews from another source, and you and your father's house will perish; and who knows, if for such a time as this you were placed in the palace."

יד כִּי אִם־הַחֲרֵשׁ תַּחֲרִישִׁי בָּעֵת הַזֹּאת רֶוַח וְהַצָּלָה יַעֲמוֹד לַיְּהוּדִים מִמָּקוֹם אַחֵר וְאַתְּ וּבֵית־אָבִיךְ תֹּאבֵדוּ וּמִי יוֹדֵעַ אִם־לְעֵת כָּזֹאת הִגַּעַתְּ לַמַּלְכוּת:

KEE im ha-kha-RAYSH ta-kha-REE-shee ba-AYT ha-ZOT RE-vakh v'-ha-tza-LAH ya-a-MOD la-y'-hu-DEEM mi-ma-KOM a-KHAYR v'-AT u-VAYT a-VEEKH to-VAY-du u-MEE yo-DAY-a im l'-AYT ka-ZOT hi-GA-at la-mal-KHUT

4:14 At such a time as this *Mordechai*'s inspiring words move *Esther* to courageously step up and defend her people. *Mordechai* does not say, "If you are silent now, then we are all doomed," because he knows that the God of Israel will never forsake His people. Instead, *Mordechai* empowers *Esther* to take a leading

Esther
CHAPTER 4

15 *Esther* then sent back this message to *Mordechai*:

16 "Go, gather all the Jews who are found in Shushan, and fast on my behalf. Do not eat or drink for three days, night and day. Me and my maidservants will also fast. I will then approach the king, though it is against the law, and if I will perish, I will perish."

טו וַתֹּאמֶר אֶסְתֵּר לְהָשִׁיב אֶל־מָרְדֳּכָי:

טז לֵךְ כְּנוֹס אֶת־כָּל־הַיְּהוּדִים הַנִּמְצְאִים בְּשׁוּשָׁן וְצוּמוּ עָלַי וְאַל־תֹּאכְלוּ וְאַל־תִּשְׁתּוּ שְׁלֹשֶׁת יָמִים לַיְלָה וָיוֹם גַּם־אֲנִי וְנַעֲרֹתַי אָצוּם כֵּן וּבְכֵן אָבוֹא אֶל־הַמֶּלֶךְ אֲשֶׁר לֹא־כַדָּת וְכַאֲשֶׁר אָבַדְתִּי אָבָדְתִּי:

LAYKH k'-NOS et kol ha-y'-hu-DEEM ha-nim-tz'-EEM b'-shu-SHAN v'-TZU-mu a-LAI v'-al to-kh'-LU v'-al tish-TU sh'-LO-shet ya-MEEM LAI-lah va-YOM gam a-NEE v'-na-a-ro-TAI a-TZUM KAYN uv-KHAYN a-VO el ha-ME-lekh a-SHER lo kha-DAT v'-kha-a-SHER a-VAD-tee a-VAD-tee

17 *Mordechai* went and did just as *Esther* had commanded him.

יז וַיַּעֲבֹר מָרְדֳּכָי וַיַּעַשׂ כְּכֹל אֲשֶׁר־צִוְּתָה עָלָיו אֶסְתֵּר:

4:16 If I will perish, I will perish *Esther's* acceptance of the perilous mission ahead of her, risking her own life for the sake of her nation, is one of the most stirring moments in the *Megilla*. Because of this act, *Esther* has served as a model for others to be willing to risk their lives in order to save the Jewish people. A striking modern example is Major Ro'i Klein, who, during the second Lebanon War in 2006, jumped on a grenade to prevent it from killing his comrades. Dying with the holy words of *Shema Yisrael* (שמע ישראל), "Hear O Israel, *Hashem* is Our God, *Hashem* is One," on his lips, Ro'i Klein sacrificed his life to save other soldiers who were fighting for the Land of Israel and the People of Israel.

role in the redemption, and not to sit quietly on the sidelines as it unfolds. In every generation there are those who threaten the existence of the Nation of Israel. Ultimately, *Hashem* will defend His people and His land, but is up to each individual to decide if he or she will stand up, as Queen *Esther* did, on behalf of Israel. Fortunately, we are living in a generation when so many Jews and non-Jews are inspired by this verse to stand with the Jewish People and the State of Israel.

CHAPTER 5
פרק ה

CHAPTER 5

ON THE THIRD DAY OF THE FAST, *ESTHER* APPEARS BEFORE the king who extends his scepter towards her. Ahasuerus asks *Esther* what her request is; he will grant her up to half the kingdom. In response, *Esther* invites Ahasuerus and Haman to a feast that day. At the feast, Ahasuerus repeats his question and *Esther* invites Ahasuerus and Haman to a second feast the following day. Haman leaves the feast in good spirits, which dissipate as soon as he sees *Mordechai* who won't bow before him. Haman arrives home, where he relates to his family how his prestigious position means nothing to him as long as *Mordechai* is still around. His wife, Zeresh, advises him to build a tall gallows and ask the king for special permission to hang *Mordechai* on it. Once *Mordechai* is gone, he will truly be able to enjoy the queen's feast the next day. Haman agrees, and the gallows are prepared.

1   It was on the third day that *Esther* dressed herself in royal clothing and stood in the inner courtyard of the king's palace, across from hte king's chamber. The king was sitting on his royal throne in the royal chamber facing the entrance of the room.

א וַיְהִי בַּיּוֹם הַשְּׁלִישִׁי וַתִּלְבַּשׁ אֶסְתֵּר מַלְכוּת וַתַּעֲמֹד בַּחֲצַר בֵּית־הַמֶּלֶךְ הַפְּנִימִית נֹכַח בֵּית הַמֶּלֶךְ וְהַמֶּלֶךְ יוֹשֵׁב עַל־כִּסֵּא מַלְכוּתוֹ בְּבֵית הַמַּלְכוּת נֹכַח פֶּתַח הַבָּיִת:

2   When the king noticed Queen *Esther* standing in the courtyard, she found favor in his eyes. The king extended the golden scepter that was in his hand to *Esther*, and *Esther* drew close and touched the top of the scepter.

ב וַיְהִי כִרְאוֹת הַמֶּלֶךְ אֶת־אֶסְתֵּר הַמַּלְכָּה עֹמֶדֶת בֶּחָצֵר נָשְׂאָה חֵן בְּעֵינָיו וַיּוֹשֶׁט הַמֶּלֶךְ לְאֶסְתֵּר אֶת־שַׁרְבִיט הַזָּהָב אֲשֶׁר בְּיָדוֹ וַתִּקְרַב אֶסְתֵּר וַתִּגַּע בְּרֹאשׁ הַשַּׁרְבִיט:

Esther
CHAPTER 5

3 The king said to her, "What can I do for you Queen *Esther*? What is your request? Up to half of the kingdom and it will be granted to you."

va-YO-mer LAH ha-ME-lekh mah LAKH es-TAYR ha-mal-KAH u-mah ba-ka-sha-TAYKH ad kha-TZEE ha-mal-KHUT v'-yi-na-TAYN LAKH

4 *Esther* said, "If it pleases the king, let the king and Haman come today to the feast that I have prepared for him."

5 The kind then said, "Quickly see to it that Haman does that which Queen *Esther* has requested. The king and Haman then came to the feast that *Esther* prepared.

6 The king said to *Esther* during the feast of wine, "What is your wish, and it will be fulfilled. What is your request? Up to half of the kingdom, and it will be granted."

7 *Esther* responded and said, "My wish and my request,

אסתר · 34
פרק ה

ג וַיֹּאמֶר לָהּ הַמֶּלֶךְ מַה־לָּךְ אֶסְתֵּר הַמַּלְכָּה וּמַה־בַּקָּשָׁתֵךְ עַד־חֲצִי הַמַּלְכוּת וְיִנָּתֵן לָךְ׃

ד וַתֹּאמֶר אֶסְתֵּר אִם־עַל־הַמֶּלֶךְ טוֹב יָבוֹא הַמֶּלֶךְ וְהָמָן הַיּוֹם אֶל־הַמִּשְׁתֶּה אֲשֶׁר־עָשִׂיתִי לוֹ׃

ה וַיֹּאמֶר הַמֶּלֶךְ מַהֲרוּ אֶת־הָמָן לַעֲשׂוֹת אֶת־דְּבַר אֶסְתֵּר וַיָּבֹא הַמֶּלֶךְ וְהָמָן אֶל־הַמִּשְׁתֶּה אֲשֶׁר־עָשְׂתָה אֶסְתֵּר׃

ו וַיֹּאמֶר הַמֶּלֶךְ לְאֶסְתֵּר בְּמִשְׁתֵּה הַיַּיִן מַה־שְּׁאֵלָתֵךְ וְיִנָּתֵן לָךְ וּמַה־בַּקָּשָׁתֵךְ עַד־חֲצִי הַמַּלְכוּת וְתֵעָשׂ׃

ז וַתַּעַן אֶסְתֵּר וַתֹּאמַר שְׁאֵלָתִי וּבַקָּשָׁתִי׃

5:3 Up to half of the kingdom When Ahasuerus offered *Esther* up to half of the kingdom, this was not merely an exaggerated show of generosity, but it referred to a specific geographic location. *Rashi* notes that the halfway mark of Ahasuerus' empire was Jerusalem. Ahasuerus tells *Esther* that he is willing to do anything to make her happy, short of allowing the rebuilding of the Temple in *Yerushalayim*. Although Cyrus, his predecessor, had allowed the Children of Israel to return to the Land of Israel and begin reconstruction of the *Beit Hamikdash*, Ahasuerus was adamantly against it. Ironically, according to Jewish tradition it was his son Darius, born to him by *Esther*, who allowed the construction of the *Beit Hamikdash* to be completed.

35 • *Esther*

CHAPTER 5

אסתר
פרק ה

8 If I have found favor in the king's eyes and if it pleases the king to bestow my wish and my request, let the king and Haman come to the feast that I will prepare for them tomorrow and I will do the king's bidding."

ח אִם־מָצָאתִי חֵן בְּעֵינֵי הַמֶּלֶךְ וְאִם־עַל־הַמֶּלֶךְ טוֹב לָתֵת אֶת־שְׁאֵלָתִי וְלַעֲשׂוֹת אֶת־בַּקָּשָׁתִי יָבוֹא הַמֶּלֶךְ וְהָמָן אֶל־הַמִּשְׁתֶּה אֲשֶׁר אֶעֱשֶׂה לָהֶם וּמָחָר אֶעֱשֶׂה כִּדְבַר הַמֶּלֶךְ:

9 Haman went out on that day joyful and elated. Yet, when Haman saw *Mordechai* in the gate of the king and he did not rise or move before him, Haman became full of fury.

ט וַיֵּצֵא הָמָן בַּיּוֹם הַהוּא שָׂמֵחַ וְטוֹב לֵב וְכִרְאוֹת הָמָן אֶת־מָרְדֳּכַי בְּשַׁעַר הַמֶּלֶךְ וְלֹא־קָם וְלֹא־זָע מִמֶּנּוּ וַיִּמָּלֵא הָמָן עַל־מָרְדֳּכַי חֵמָה:

10 Haman restrained himself and came home. He sent for and convened his loved ones and his wife Zeresh.

י וַיִּתְאַפַּק הָמָן וַיָּבוֹא אֶל־בֵּיתוֹ וַיִּשְׁלַח וַיָּבֵא אֶת־אֹהֲבָיו וְאֶת־זֶרֶשׁ אִשְׁתּוֹ:

11 Haman described all of his honor and wealth, as well as his many sons and how the king promoted him over the other ministers and royal servants.

יא וַיְסַפֵּר לָהֶם הָמָן אֶת־כְּבוֹד עָשְׁרוֹ וְרֹב בָּנָיו וְאֵת כָּל־אֲשֶׁר גִּדְּלוֹ הַמֶּלֶךְ וְאֵת אֲשֶׁר נִשְּׂאוֹ עַל־הַשָּׂרִים וְעַבְדֵי הַמֶּלֶךְ:

vai-sa-PAYR la-HEM ha-MAN et k'-VOD osh-RO v'-ROV ba-NAV v'-AYT kol a-SHER gi-d'-LO ha-ME-lekh v'-AYT a-SHER ni-s'-O al ha-sa-REEM v'-av-DAY ha-ME-lekh

5:11 Haman described all of his honor and wealth The Hebrew word for wealth is *osher*, spelled with the letter *ayin* (עושר). The Hebrew word for 'happiness' is also *osher*, but spelled with the letter *alef* (אושר). While the two words are homophones, they are not synonymous. Some people mistakenly believe that wealth leads to happiness. The Sages (Ethics of the Fathers 4:1), however, teach the exact opposite. "Who is wealthy? One who is happy with his lot." Haman is a prime example of a man who had everything including wealth, power, honor and family, as he himself recounts in these verses. Despite this, he chooses to focus on what he lacks and concludes: "Yet all this means nothing to me" (verse 13). Only when a person is happy and satisfied with the material possessions that he has, no matter their value, can he be considered truly wealthy.

Esther
CHAPTER 5

12 Furthermore, Haman exclaimed to them, "Queen *Esther* did not bring anyone else to join with the king at the feast that she prepared except for me, and I was invited to join her with the king tomorrow as well.

13 Yet, all of this has no value to me as long I see *Mordechai* the Jew sitting in the gate of the king."

14 His wife Zeresh and all his loved ones responded, "They should prepare gallows fifty *amah* cubits high and in the morning you should tell the king that they should hang *Mordechai* upon it. Then, go with the king to the feast joyously." This suggestion pleased Haman, and he prepared the gallows.

אסתר · 36
פרק ה

יב וַיֹּאמֶר הָמָן אַף לֹא־הֵבִיאָה אֶסְתֵּר הַמַּלְכָּה עִם־הַמֶּלֶךְ אֶל־הַמִּשְׁתֶּה אֲשֶׁר־עָשָׂתָה כִּי אִם־אוֹתִי וְגַם־לְמָחָר אֲנִי קָרוּא־לָהּ עִם־הַמֶּלֶךְ:

יג וְכָל־זֶה אֵינֶנּוּ שֹׁוֶה לִי בְּכָל־עֵת אֲשֶׁר אֲנִי רֹאֶה אֶת־מָרְדֳּכַי הַיְּהוּדִי יוֹשֵׁב בְּשַׁעַר הַמֶּלֶךְ:

יד וַתֹּאמֶר לוֹ זֶרֶשׁ אִשְׁתּוֹ וְכָל־אֹהֲבָיו יַעֲשׂוּ־עֵץ גָּבֹהַּ חֲמִשִּׁים אַמָּה וּבַבֹּקֶר אֱמֹר לַמֶּלֶךְ וְיִתְלוּ אֶת־מָרְדֳּכַי עָלָיו וּבֹא־עִם־הַמֶּלֶךְ אֶל־הַמִּשְׁתֶּה שָׂמֵחַ וַיִּיטַב הַדָּבָר לִפְנֵי הָמָן וַיַּעַשׂ הָעֵץ:

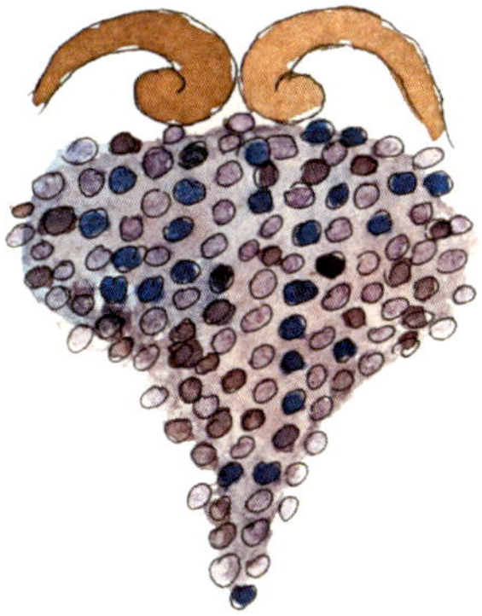

CHAPTER 6
פרק ו

CHAPTER 6

THE NIGHT FOLLOWING *ESTHER*'S FIRST FEAST, AHASUERUS can't sleep. He asks that his book of records be read to him, and is surprised to learn that *Mordechai* has never been rewarded for saving his life years earlier. At that moment, Haman arrives in the courtyard to ask permission from the king to hang *Mordechai*. Ahasuerus asks Haman what he deems a sufficient reward for someone the king wishes to honor. Haman, assuming Ahasuerus is referring to him, suggests that such a person should don royal clothing, ride on the royal horse and be led through the streets of Shushan with a herald proclaiming, "So shall be done to the man the king wishes to honor!" Ahasuerus commands Haman to do as he described – to *Mordechai*. Haman obeys, and returns home downcast. He describes the events of his day to his family, who reply that if *Mordechai* is a Jew and has started to prevail, Haman will not be able to vanquish him. As they are talking, the king's officers come to bring Haman to the queen's party.

1 On that night the king could not sleep, so called for the scroll of records, the archives, to be read before the king.

א בַּלַּיְלָה הַהוּא נָדְדָה שְׁנַת הַמֶּלֶךְ וַיֹּאמֶר לְהָבִיא אֶת־סֵפֶר הַזִּכְרֹנוֹת דִּבְרֵי הַיָּמִים וַיִּהְיוּ נִקְרָאִים לִפְנֵי הַמֶּלֶךְ׃

ba-LAI-lah ha-HU na-d'-DAH sh'-NAT ha-ME-lekh va-YO-mer l'-ha-VEE et SAY-fer ha-zikh-ro-NOT div-RAY ha-ya-MEEM va-yih-YU nik-ra-EEM lif-NAY ha-ME-lekh

6:1 On that night Upon careful reading of *Megillat Esther*, it becomes clear "that night" was the second night of *Pesach*. Since Haman's letters had been sent out on the thirteenth day of *Nisan*, and *Esther* called for three days

Esther
CHAPTER 6

2 It was found recorded that *Mordechai* reported that Bigthana and Teresh, two royal eunuchs, who guarded the entrance to the king's chamber, sought to assassinate King Ahasuerus.

3 The king asked, "What honor and grandeur has been done for *Mordechai* for this?" The young men of the king, who served him replied that nothing had been done.

4 The king asked, "Who is in the courtyard?" Haman had come to the outer courtyard of the palace to discuss hanging *Mordechai* on the gallows that he had prepared.

5 The king's young servants replied, "Behold, Haman stands in the courtyard." The king then said, "Let him come in."

6 Haman entered and the king asked, "What should be done for a man that the king wishes to honor?" Haman thought in his heart, "Who would the king wish to honor more than me?"

ב וַיִּמָּצֵא כָתוּב אֲשֶׁר הִגִּיד מָרְדֳּכַי עַל־בִּגְתָנָא וָתֶרֶשׁ שְׁנֵי סָרִיסֵי הַמֶּלֶךְ מִשֹּׁמְרֵי הַסַּף אֲשֶׁר בִּקְשׁוּ לִשְׁלֹחַ יָד בַּמֶּלֶךְ אֲחַשְׁוֵרוֹשׁ:

ג וַיֹּאמֶר הַמֶּלֶךְ מַה־נַּעֲשָׂה יְקָר וּגְדוּלָּה לְמָרְדֳּכַי עַל־זֶה וַיֹּאמְרוּ נַעֲרֵי הַמֶּלֶךְ מְשָׁרְתָיו לֹא־נַעֲשָׂה עִמּוֹ דָּבָר:

ד וַיֹּאמֶר הַמֶּלֶךְ מִי בֶחָצֵר וְהָמָן בָּא לַחֲצַר בֵּית־הַמֶּלֶךְ הַחִיצוֹנָה לֵאמֹר לַמֶּלֶךְ לִתְלוֹת אֶת־מָרְדֳּכַי עַל־הָעֵץ אֲשֶׁר־הֵכִין לוֹ:

ה וַיֹּאמְרוּ נַעֲרֵי הַמֶּלֶךְ אֵלָיו הִנֵּה הָמָן עֹמֵד בֶּחָצֵר וַיֹּאמֶר הַמֶּלֶךְ יָבוֹא:

ו וַיָּבוֹא הָמָן וַיֹּאמֶר לוֹ הַמֶּלֶךְ מַה־לַּעֲשׂוֹת בָּאִישׁ אֲשֶׁר הַמֶּלֶךְ חָפֵץ בִּיקָרוֹ וַיֹּאמֶר הָמָן בְּלִבּוֹ לְמִי יַחְפֹּץ הַמֶּלֶךְ לַעֲשׂוֹת יְקָר יוֹתֵר מִמֶּנִּי:

of fasting, the first banquet took place on the sixteenth of *Nisan*. The Talmud (*Megilla* 16a) relates that when Haman looked for *Mordechai* in order to lead him around the city, he found the Jewish leader teaching the laws of the offerings brought in the *Beit Hamikdash* on *Pesach* in Jerusalem. When granted permission to rebuild the *Beit Hamikdash* by Cyrus, the Jews, unfortunately, did not heed the call, and only a small minority returned to *Yerushalayim*. Hoping to rectify this mistake which potentially brought about Haman's decree of annihilation, *Mordechai* was teaching longingly about the *Beit Hamikdash* and its laws. Though in exile, the Jews have remained connected to *Yerushalayim* and the Holy Temple through the study of *Torah*, in the hopes of rebuilding it once again.

41 • *Esther*
CHAPTER 6

אסתר
פרק ו

7 Haman replied to the king, "For the man that the king wishes to honor,

ז וַיֹּאמֶר הָמָן אֶל־הַמֶּלֶךְ אִישׁ אֲשֶׁר הַמֶּלֶךְ חָפֵץ בִּיקָרוֹ:

8 they should bring the royal clothing that was worn by the king and the horse that the king rode upon with a royal crown upon its head.

ח יָבִיאוּ לְבוּשׁ מַלְכוּת אֲשֶׁר לָבַשׁ־בּוֹ הַמֶּלֶךְ וְסוּס אֲשֶׁר רָכַב עָלָיו הַמֶּלֶךְ וַאֲשֶׁר נִתַּן כֶּתֶר מַלְכוּת בְּרֹאשׁוֹ:

9 The clothing and the horse should be delivered by one of the king's most important ministers. Let them dress the man whom the king desires to honor, and they should lead him as he rides on the horse through the streets of the city. They should declare before him, 'This is what is done for the man whom the king wishes to honor!'"

ט וְנָתוֹן הַלְּבוּשׁ וְהַסּוּס עַל־יַד־אִישׁ מִשָּׂרֵי הַמֶּלֶךְ הַפַּרְתְּמִים וְהִלְבִּישׁוּ אֶת־הָאִישׁ אֲשֶׁר הַמֶּלֶךְ חָפֵץ בִּיקָרוֹ וְהִרְכִּיבֻהוּ עַל־הַסּוּס בִּרְחוֹב הָעִיר וְקָרְאוּ לְפָנָיו כָּכָה יֵעָשֶׂה לָאִישׁ אֲשֶׁר הַמֶּלֶךְ חָפֵץ בִּיקָרוֹ:

10 The king then said to Haman, "Quickly take the clothing and the horse as you recommended, and do so for *Mordechai* the Jew, who is sitting at the king's gate. Do not neglect anything that you suggested!"

י וַיֹּאמֶר הַמֶּלֶךְ לְהָמָן מַהֵר קַח אֶת־הַלְּבוּשׁ וְאֶת־הַסּוּס כַּאֲשֶׁר דִּבַּרְתָּ וַעֲשֵׂה־כֵן לְמָרְדֳּכַי הַיְּהוּדִי הַיּוֹשֵׁב בְּשַׁעַר הַמֶּלֶךְ אַל־תַּפֵּל דָּבָר מִכֹּל אֲשֶׁר דִּבַּרְתָּ:

va-YO-mer ha-ME-lekh l'-ha-MAN ma-HAYR KAKH et ha-l'-VUSH v'-et ha-SUS ka-a-SHER di-BAR-ta va-a-say KHAYN l'-mor-d'-KHAI ha-y'-hu-DEE ha-yo-SHAYV b'-SHA-ar ha-ME-lekh al ta-PAYL da-VAR mi-KOL a-SHER di-BAR-ta

6:10 *Mordechai* the Jew The chosen people have many biblical names, including 'Hebrews' and 'Children of Israel' to name a few. What is the origin of the title 'Jew', or, in Hebrew, *Yehudi* (יהודי)? The term is first employed during the Babylonian exile, as can be seen in this verse and in the books of *Daniel* and *Ezra*. Historically, this name indicated an association with the tribe of *Yehuda* (יהודה), from which most of the Babylonian exiles descended. However, the name actually derives from the Hebrew root which means to 'praise' or 'give thanks',

Esther
CHAPTER 6

11 Haman took the clothing and the horse, and dressed *Mordechai*. He led him on a horse through the streets of the city, and called out before him, "This is what is done for the man whom the king wishes to honor!"

12 *Mordechai* then returned to the king's gate, and Haman quickly returned home in a state of mourning and with his head covered.

13 Haman related to his wife Zeresh and all his loved ones all that happened to him. His advisors and his wife Zeresh said to him, "If *Mordechai*, before whom you have started to fall, is of Jewish descent, you will not be able to overcome him, but will certainly fall before him.

14 As they were speaking with him, the king's eunuchs arrived and rushed to bring Haman to the feast that *Esther* prepared.

יא וַיִּקַּח הָמָן אֶת־הַלְּבוּשׁ וְאֶת־הַסּוּס וַיַּלְבֵּשׁ אֶת־מָרְדֳּכָי וַיַּרְכִּיבֵהוּ בִּרְחוֹב הָעִיר וַיִּקְרָא לְפָנָיו כָּכָה יֵעָשֶׂה לָאִישׁ אֲשֶׁר הַמֶּלֶךְ חָפֵץ בִּיקָרוֹ:

יב וַיָּשָׁב מָרְדֳּכַי אֶל־שַׁעַר הַמֶּלֶךְ וְהָמָן נִדְחַף אֶל־בֵּיתוֹ אָבֵל וַחֲפוּי רֹאשׁ:

יג וַיְסַפֵּר הָמָן לְזֶרֶשׁ אִשְׁתּוֹ וּלְכָל־אֹהֲבָיו אֵת כָּל־אֲשֶׁר קָרָהוּ וַיֹּאמְרוּ לוֹ חֲכָמָיו וְזֶרֶשׁ אִשְׁתּוֹ אִם מִזֶּרַע הַיְּהוּדִים מָרְדֳּכַי אֲשֶׁר הַחִלּוֹתָ לִנְפֹּל לְפָנָיו לֹא־תוּכַל לוֹ כִּי־נָפוֹל תִּפּוֹל לְפָנָיו:

יד עוֹדָם מְדַבְּרִים עִמּוֹ וְסָרִיסֵי הַמֶּלֶךְ הִגִּיעוּ וַיַּבְהִלוּ לְהָבִיא אֶת־הָמָן אֶל־הַמִּשְׁתֶּה אֲשֶׁר־עָשְׂתָה אֶסְתֵּר:

as it says that *Leah* "conceived again and bore a son, and declared, 'This time I will praise *Hashem*.' Therefore, she named him *Yehuda*" (Genesis 29:35). The name thus highlights the inherent Jewish value of gratitude to God. The fact that this collective name was given in exile shows that sometimes one has to travel far away to discover who they really are.

CHAPTER 7
פרק ז

CHAPTER 7

AT *ESTHER*'S SECOND FEAST, AHASUERUS AGAIN ASKS *Esther* what is it that she desires. *Esther* replies that her request is her life and the life of her nation, which have been sold for annihilation. Shocked, Ahasuerus, asks her to identify the person who would dare to do such a thing. *Esther* replies that it is the evil Haman, and Haman is flabbergasted. Ahasuerus is furious and goes out to his garden, and Haman begs *Esther* for his life. When Ahasuerus returns, he finds Haman prostrate on *Esther's* couch, leading Ahasuerus to assume that Haman is trying to ravage the queen. Harbonah, one of the king's servants, informs the king that Haman has made a tree on which to hang *Mordechai*, who had saved the king's life. Ahasuerus orders that Haman be hung on that very tree instead of *Mordechai*.

1 The king and Haman came to drink with Queen *Esther*.

א וַיָּבֹא הַמֶּלֶךְ וְהָמָן לִשְׁתּוֹת עִם־אֶסְתֵּר הַמַּלְכָּה:

va-ya-VO ha-ME-lekh v'-ha-MAN lish-TOT im es-TAYR ha-mal-KAH

7:1 The king and Haman Why does *Esther* invite Haman to her banquet with Ahasuerus? One suggestion is that, as long as the Jewish people knew that they had *Esther* in the palace, they were counting on her to reverse Haman's evil decree. Yet *Esther* wanted the people themselves to fully repent. Inviting Haman made it appear that she was abandoning her people and aligning with the wicked Haman. At that point, the terrified nation called out to *Hashem* with a new intensity that merited salvation. Throughout the ages, true redemption arrives when we realize that we have no one to rely on aside from God above.

Esther
CHAPTER 7

2 On the second day of the drinking feast, the king again asked *Esther*, "What is your wish Queen *Esther*, and it will be granted to you. What is your request? Up to half of the kingdom, and it will be granted."

ב וַיֹּאמֶר הַמֶּלֶךְ לְאֶסְתֵּר גַּם בַּיּוֹם הַשֵּׁנִי בְּמִשְׁתֵּה הַיַּיִן מַה־שְּׁאֵלָתֵךְ אֶסְתֵּר הַמַּלְכָּה וְתִנָּתֵן לָךְ וּמַה־בַּקָּשָׁתֵךְ עַד־חֲצִי הַמַּלְכוּת וְתֵעָשׂ׃

va-YO-mer ha-ME-lekh l'-es-TAYR GAM ba-YOM ha-shay-NEE b'-mish-TAYH ha-YA-yin mah sh'-ay-la-TAYKH es-TAYR ha-mal-KAH v'-ti-NA-tayn LAKH u-mah ba-ka-sha-TAYKH ad kha-TZEE ha-mal-KHUT v'-tay-AS

3 Queen *Esther* responded and replied, "If I have found favor in the eyes of the king and if it pleases the king, let my life be given to me as my wish and my people as my request.

ג וַתַּעַן אֶסְתֵּר הַמַּלְכָּה וַתֹּאמַר אִם־מָצָאתִי חֵן בְּעֵינֶיךָ הַמֶּלֶךְ וְאִם־עַל־הַמֶּלֶךְ טוֹב תִּנָּתֶן־לִי נַפְשִׁי בִּשְׁאֵלָתִי וְעַמִּי בְּבַקָּשָׁתִי׃

4 For I and my people have been sold to be destroyed, murdered, and annihilated. If we would have only been sold as slaves and maidservants, I would have remained silent, for then our pain would not be worth troubling the king."

ד כִּי נִמְכַּרְנוּ אֲנִי וְעַמִּי לְהַשְׁמִיד לַהֲרוֹג וּלְאַבֵּד וְאִלּוּ לַעֲבָדִים וְלִשְׁפָחוֹת נִמְכַּרְנוּ הֶחֱרַשְׁתִּי כִּי אֵין הַצָּר שֹׁוֶה בְּנֵזֶק הַמֶּלֶךְ׃

7:2 The drinking feast The holiday of *Purim* is celebrated with wine to commemorate the salvation of the Jewish people that came through wine. Vashti's downfall, which made way for *Esther* to become queen, happened when the king was intoxicated, and Haman's downfall also took place at a drinking feast. We can learn a powerful lesson from wine which is made from grapes, one of the seven special agricultural products of *Eretz Yisrael*. Grapes must be totally crushed in order to produce wine. This is also the case for righteous individuals. Only through trials and tribulations is our true potential brought to fruition. *Esther* is a prime example of this. Orphaned at a young age and taken by force to the palace, it is precisely these trying circumstances that set the stage for her heroism, which emerges through the consumption of wine.

47 · *Esther*
CHAPTER 7

5 King Ahasuerus said to Queen *Esther*, "Who is he and where is he who desires to do this?"

6 "The man who is the adversary and enemy is this evil Haman!" *Esther* said. Haman quivered from before the king and the queen.

7 The king then arose in anger from the wine feast to the palace garden. Haman stood to beg for his life from Queen *Esther* since he saw that the king resolved that he was evil.

8 The king returned from the palace garden to the chamber where the drinking feast was being held and Haman had fallen upon the couch that *Esther* was on. He exclaimed, "will you also ravish the queen while I am in the house?" Once the words emerged from the mouth of the king, they covered Haman's face.

9 Harbonah, one of the eunuchs, said before the king, "Also, there is the fifty *amah* tall gallows that Haman prepared for *Mordechai*, who spoke up on behalf of the king, standing in Haman's house." The king said, "Hang him on it!"

10 They hanged Haman on the gallows that was prepared for *Mordechai*, and the anger of the king subsided.

אסתר
פרק ז

ה וַיֹּאמֶר הַמֶּלֶךְ אֲחַשְׁוֵרוֹשׁ וַיֹּאמֶר לְאֶסְתֵּר הַמַּלְכָּה מִי הוּא זֶה וְאֵי־זֶה הוּא אֲשֶׁר־מְלָאוֹ לִבּוֹ לַעֲשׂוֹת כֵּן:

ו וַתֹּאמֶר־אֶסְתֵּר אִישׁ צַר וְאוֹיֵב הָמָן הָרָע הַזֶּה וְהָמָן נִבְעַת מִלִּפְנֵי הַמֶּלֶךְ וְהַמַּלְכָּה:

ז וְהַמֶּלֶךְ קָם בַּחֲמָתוֹ מִמִּשְׁתֵּה הַיַּיִן אֶל־גִּנַּת הַבִּיתָן וְהָמָן עָמַד לְבַקֵּשׁ עַל־נַפְשׁוֹ מֵאֶסְתֵּר הַמַּלְכָּה כִּי רָאָה כִּי־כָלְתָה אֵלָיו הָרָעָה מֵאֵת הַמֶּלֶךְ:

ח וְהַמֶּלֶךְ שָׁב מִגִּנַּת הַבִּיתָן אֶל־בֵּית מִשְׁתֵּה הַיַּיִן וְהָמָן נֹפֵל עַל־הַמִּטָּה אֲשֶׁר אֶסְתֵּר עָלֶיהָ וַיֹּאמֶר הַמֶּלֶךְ הֲגַם לִכְבּוֹשׁ אֶת־הַמַּלְכָּה עִמִּי בַּבָּיִת הַדָּבָר יָצָא מִפִּי הַמֶּלֶךְ וּפְנֵי הָמָן חָפוּ:

ט וַיֹּאמֶר חַרְבוֹנָה אֶחָד מִן־הַסָּרִיסִים לִפְנֵי הַמֶּלֶךְ גַּם הִנֵּה־הָעֵץ אֲשֶׁר־עָשָׂה הָמָן לְמָרְדֳּכַי אֲשֶׁר דִּבֶּר־טוֹב עַל־הַמֶּלֶךְ עֹמֵד בְּבֵית הָמָן גָּבֹהַּ חֲמִשִּׁים אַמָּה וַיֹּאמֶר הַמֶּלֶךְ תְּלֻהוּ עָלָיו:

י וַיִּתְלוּ אֶת־הָמָן עַל־הָעֵץ אֲשֶׁר־הֵכִין לְמָרְדֳּכָי וַחֲמַת הַמֶּלֶךְ שָׁכָכָה:

CHAPTER 8
פרק ח

CHAPTER 8

AHASUERUS GIVES HAMAN'S ESTATE TO *ESTHER* AND his signet ring to *Mordechai*. *Esther* again pleads before the king to abolish Haman's evil decree of destruction against the Jewish people. Ahasuerus replies that even he cannot revoke the old edict, but can issue a new decree for the benefit of the Jews, since a decree that has been sealed with the king's ring cannot be cancelled. On the 23rd of *Sivan*, *Mordechai* issues a new decree that grants the Jewish people permission to defend themselves from those who will rise up against them on the 13th of *Adar*. *Mordechai* leaves the palace wearing royal garments, and Shushan rejoices. Wherever news of the decree reaches, the Jews respond with joy and feasting.

1 On that very day, King Ahasuerus gave the estate of Haman, the enemy fo the Jews, to Queen *Esther*. *Mordechai* came before the king since *Esther* informed him of his relationship to her.

א בַּיּוֹם הַהוּא נָתַן הַמֶּלֶךְ אֲחַשְׁוֵרוֹשׁ לְאֶסְתֵּר הַמַּלְכָּה אֶת־בֵּית הָמָן צֹרֵר היהודיים [הַיְּהוּדִים] וּמָרְדֳּכַי בָּא לִפְנֵי הַמֶּלֶךְ כִּי־הִגִּידָה אֶסְתֵּר מַה הוּא־לָהּ:

2 The king removed his signet ring that was taken from Haman, and gave it to *Mordechai*. *Esther* then appointed *Mordechai* to be in charge of Haman's estate.

ב וַיָּסַר הַמֶּלֶךְ אֶת־טַבַּעְתּוֹ אֲשֶׁר הֶעֱבִיר מֵהָמָן וַיִּתְּנָהּ לְמָרְדֳּכָי וַתָּשֶׂם אֶסְתֵּר אֶת־מָרְדֳּכַי עַל־בֵּית הָמָן:

3 *Esther* continued to speak before the king. She fell before his feet and cried as she beseeched him to remove the evil decree of Haman the Agagite and his plan that was designed regarding the Jews.

ג וַתּוֹסֶף אֶסְתֵּר וַתְּדַבֵּר לִפְנֵי הַמֶּלֶךְ וַתִּפֹּל לִפְנֵי רַגְלָיו וַתֵּבְךְּ וַתִּתְחַנֶּן־לוֹ לְהַעֲבִיר אֶת־רָעַת הָמָן הָאֲגָגִי וְאֵת מַחֲשַׁבְתּוֹ אֲשֶׁר חָשַׁב עַל־הַיְּהוּדִים:

Esther
CHAPTER 8

4 The king extended the golden scepter to *Esther*, and she rose and stood before the king.

5 She said, "If it is pleasing to the king and I have found favor before him. If the matter is proper before the king, and I am pleasing in his eyes, let it be written that the letters declaring the plot of Haman, son of Hammedatha the Agagite, in which he had written to destroy the Jews that are in all of the provinces of the king be rescinded.

6 For, how am I able to bear the evil decree that will fall upon my people? How can I witness the destruction of my people?"

7 King Ahasuerus replied to Queen *Esther* and *Mordechai* the Jew, "Behold, I gave the estate of Haman to *Esther* and hanged him on the gallows because he directed his hand against the Jews.

8 You can write about the Jews that which is fitting in your eyes in the name of the king and sign it with the king's signet ring. For a letter written in the name of the king and signed with the king's signet ring cannot be rescinded.

52 · אסתר
פרק ח

ד וַיּוֹשֶׁט הַמֶּלֶךְ לְאֶסְתֵּר אֵת שַׁרְבִט הַזָּהָב וַתָּקָם אֶסְתֵּר וַתַּעֲמֹד לִפְנֵי הַמֶּלֶךְ:

ה וַתֹּאמֶר אִם־עַל־הַמֶּלֶךְ טוֹב וְאִם־מָצָאתִי חֵן לְפָנָיו וְכָשֵׁר הַדָּבָר לִפְנֵי הַמֶּלֶךְ וְטוֹבָה אֲנִי בְּעֵינָיו יִכָּתֵב לְהָשִׁיב אֶת־הַסְּפָרִים מַחֲשֶׁבֶת הָמָן בֶּן־הַמְּדָתָא הָאֲגָגִי אֲשֶׁר כָּתַב לְאַבֵּד אֶת־הַיְּהוּדִים אֲשֶׁר בְּכָל־מְדִינוֹת הַמֶּלֶךְ:

ו כִּי אֵיכָכָה אוּכַל וְרָאִיתִי בָּרָעָה אֲשֶׁר־יִמְצָא אֶת־עַמִּי וְאֵיכָכָה אוּכַל וְרָאִיתִי בְּאָבְדַן מוֹלַדְתִּי:

ז וַיֹּאמֶר הַמֶּלֶךְ אֲחַשְׁוֵרוֹשׁ לְאֶסְתֵּר הַמַּלְכָּה וּלְמָרְדֳּכַי הַיְּהוּדִי הִנֵּה בֵית־הָמָן נָתַתִּי לְאֶסְתֵּר וְאֹתוֹ תָּלוּ עַל־הָעֵץ עַל אֲשֶׁר־שָׁלַח יָדוֹ בַּיְּהוּדִיִּים [בַּיְּהוּדִים]:

ח וְאַתֶּם כִּתְבוּ עַל־הַיְּהוּדִים כַּטּוֹב בְּעֵינֵיכֶם בְּשֵׁם הַמֶּלֶךְ וְחִתְמוּ בְּטַבַּעַת הַמֶּלֶךְ כִּי־כְתָב אֲשֶׁר־נִכְתָּב בְּשֵׁם־הַמֶּלֶךְ וְנַחְתּוֹם בְּטַבַּעַת הַמֶּלֶךְ אֵין לְהָשִׁיב:

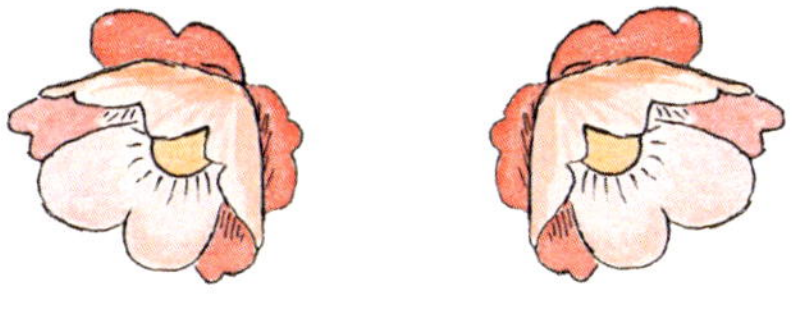

53 · *Esther*
CHAPTER 8

9 The royal scribes were called at that time in the third month, which is the month of *Sivan,* on the twenty third day. A letter was written to the Jews, the regional leaders, the provincial governors, and the ministers of the provinces that were from India to Ethiopia spanning one hundred and twenty-seven provinces, according to everything dictated by *Mordechai.* Each province according to its script and each nation in its own language. To the Jews in their own script and according to their language.

va-yi-ka-r'-U so-f'-RAY ha-ME-lekh ba-ayt ha-HEE ba-KHO-desh ha-sh'-lee-SHEE hu KHO-desh see-VAN bish-lo-SHAH v'-es-REEM BO va-yi-ka-TAYV k'-khol a-sher tzi-VAH mor-d'-KHAI el ha-y'-hu-DEEM v'-EL ha-a-khash-dar-p'-NEEM v'-ha-pa-KHOT v'-sa-RAY ha-m'-dee-NOT a-SHER may-HO-du v'-ad KUSH SHE-va v'-es-REEM u-may-AH m'-dee-NAH m'-dee-NAH um-dee-NAH kikh-ta-VAH v'-AM va-AM kil-sho-NO v'-EL ha-y'-hu-DEEM kikh-ta-VAM v'-khil-sho-NAM

אסתר
פרק ח

ט וַיִּקָּרְאוּ סֹפְרֵי־הַמֶּלֶךְ בָּעֵת־הַהִיא בַּחֹדֶשׁ הַשְּׁלִישִׁי הוּא־חֹדֶשׁ סִיוָן בִּשְׁלוֹשָׁה וְעֶשְׂרִים בּוֹ וַיִּכָּתֵב כְּכָל־אֲשֶׁר־צִוָּה מָרְדֳּכַי אֶל־הַיְּהוּדִים וְאֶל הָאֲחַשְׁדַּרְפְּנִים־וְהַפַּחוֹת וְשָׂרֵי הַמְּדִינוֹת אֲשֶׁר ׀ מֵהֹדּוּ וְעַד־כּוּשׁ שֶׁבַע וְעֶשְׂרִים וּמֵאָה מְדִינָה מְדִינָה וּמְדִינָה כִּכְתָבָהּ וְעַם וָעָם כִּלְשֹׁנוֹ וְאֶל־הַיְּהוּדִים כִּכְתָבָם וְכִלְשׁוֹנָם:

8:9 The month of *Sivan* Throughout *Megillat Esther*, the Hebrew months are referred to by both number and name. *Ramban* (Exodus 12:2) teaches that originally the months were referred to by numbers, with the first month being the month of the redemption from Egypt, in order to commemorate the Exodus from Egypt. During the Babylonian exile, however, the Jews adopted the Persian names for the months, which are used to this day. Just as the original numbering of the months included a reference to the Exodus from Egypt, the Persian names recall the return of the Jewish people from the Babylonian exile. In this way, all references to the Jewish calendar contain a subtle allusion to the first redemption from exile and the re-entry into the Land of Israel.

Esther
CHAPTER 8

10 He wrote in the name of King Ahasuerus and sealed it with the king's signet ring. He then sent the letters with the couriers on horseback, as well as riders on speedy mules born of horses.

י וַיִּכְתֹּב בְּשֵׁם הַמֶּלֶךְ אֲחַשְׁוֵרֹשׁ וַיַּחְתֹּם בְּטַבַּעַת הַמֶּלֶךְ וַיִּשְׁלַח סְפָרִים בְּיַד הָרָצִים בַּסּוּסִים רֹכְבֵי הָרֶכֶשׁ הָאֲחַשְׁתְּרָנִים בְּנֵי הָרַמָּכִים׃

11 That the king had granted permission to the Jews in every city to assemble and defend themselves, to destroy, kill, and annihilate any soldier of any nation and province that comes to terrorize them, including their children and women and to take their spoils,

יא אֲשֶׁר נָתַן הַמֶּלֶךְ לַיְּהוּדִים אֲשֶׁר בְּכָל־עִיר־וָעִיר לְהִקָּהֵל וְלַעֲמֹד עַל־נַפְשָׁם לְהַשְׁמִיד וְלַהֲרֹג וּלְאַבֵּד אֶת־כָּל־חֵיל עַם וּמְדִינָה הַצָּרִים אֹתָם טַף וְנָשִׁים וּשְׁלָלָם לָבוֹז׃

a-SHER na-TAN ha-ME-lekh la-y'-hu-DEEM a-SHER b'-khol eer va-EER l'-hi-ka-HAYL v'-la-a-MOD al naf-SHAM l'-hash-MEED v'-la-ha-ROG ul-a-BAYD et kol KHAYL AM um-dee-NAH ha-tza-REEM o-TAM TAF v'-na-SHEEM ush-la-LAM la-VOZ

12 for one day in all the king's provinces, which was the thirteenth day of the twelfth month, the month of *Adar*.

יב בְּיוֹם אֶחָד בְּכָל־מְדִינוֹת הַמֶּלֶךְ אֲחַשְׁוֵרוֹשׁ בִּשְׁלוֹשָׁה עָשָׂר לְחֹדֶשׁ שְׁנֵים־עָשָׂר הוּא־חֹדֶשׁ אֲדָר׃

13 A copy of the decree's text was distributed in every province and publicized to all the people, so that the Jews would be prepared for the upcoming day to retaliate against their enemies.

יג פַּתְשֶׁגֶן הַכְּתָב לְהִנָּתֵן דָּת בְּכָל־מְדִינָה וּמְדִינָה גָּלוּי לְכָל־הָעַמִּים וְלִהְיוֹת היהודיים [הַיְּהוּדִים] עתודים [עֲתִידִים] לַיּוֹם הַזֶּה לְהִנָּקֵם מֵאֹיְבֵיהֶם׃

8:11 Any soldier of any nation The edict clearly states that the Jews would gather in self-defense only. This is one of the foundations of Jewish military ethics. The People of Israel are required to fight wars to defend themselves and to strengthen the Promised Land, while offensive wars are not permitted. The State of Israel follows this biblical mandate. This is shown even in the name of the Jewish army – the Israel Defense Forces, or, in Hebrew, *Tz'va HaHaganah L'Yisrael* (צבא ההגנה לישראל).

55 · *Esther*
CHAPTER 8

אסתר
פרק ח

14 The couriers who rode on the speedy mules went out in a hurry and with urgency by the decree of the king, and it was distributed in the capital of Shushan.

יד הָרָצִים רֹכְבֵי הָרֶכֶשׁ הָאֲחַשְׁתְּרָנִים יָצְאוּ מְבֹהָלִים וּדְחוּפִים בִּדְבַר הַמֶּלֶךְ וְהַדָּת נִתְּנָה בְּשׁוּשַׁן הַבִּירָה:

15 *Mordechai* left from the king's presence in royal clothing made of blue and white, with a large golden crown and a robe of linen and purple and the city of Shushan was elated and joyful.

טו וּמָרְדֳּכַי יָצָא מִלִּפְנֵי הַמֶּלֶךְ בִּלְבוּשׁ מַלְכוּת תְּכֵלֶת וָחוּר וַעֲטֶרֶת זָהָב גְּדוֹלָה וְתַכְרִיךְ בּוּץ וְאַרְגָּמָן וְהָעִיר שׁוּשָׁן צָהֲלָה וְשָׂמֵחָה:

u-mor-d'-KHAI ya-TZA mi-lif-NAY ha-ME-lekh bil-VUSH mal-KHUT t'-KHAY-let va-KHUR va-a-TE-ret za-HAV g'-do-LAH v'-takh-REEKH BUTZ v'-ar-ga-MAN v'-ha-EER shu-SHAN tza-ha-LAH v'-sa-MAY-khah

16 For the Jews there was light and happiness, joy and honor.

טז לַיְּהוּדִים הָיְתָה אוֹרָה וְשִׂמְחָה וְשָׂשֹׂן וִיקָר:

la-y'-hu-DEEM ha-y'-TAH o-RAH v'-sim-KHAH v'-sa-SON vee-KAR

8:15 In royal clothing of blue and white The biblical blue color of *techelet* (תכלת) is mentioned numerous times in the Bible. One example is the cord of *techelet* which is attached to the fringes of a four-cornered garment, known as *tzitzit* (ציצית) (Numbers 15:38). *Rashi* explains that wearing this color is meant to remind us of the sky, and, by extension, *Hashem* and His constant presence in our lives. Yet, for close to fifteen hundred years, the source of this special blue dye had been lost to the world. In an exciting discovery in recent years, Israeli marine biologists, together with Talmudic researchers, identified the source of *tekhelet* as a small snail found off the coast near Haifa. Today, people are wearing *tekhelet* on their *tzitzit* for the first time in centuries. From even the smallest sea creature we continue to see the wonders of the Bible come to life in *Eretz Yisrael*.

8:16 Light and happiness In his comment on the verse "For there is a time for every season" (Ecclesiastes 8:6), the *Sforno* explains that God desires that various biblical commandments be observed at specific times of the year, since each season contains unique powers. The month of *Elul*, for example,

Esther
CHAPTER 8

56 · אסתר
פרק ח

17 In every province and every city, in any place that the word and decree of the king reached, there was happiness and joy for the Jews, a banquet and a holiday. And many of the people of the land came close to the Jews, for fear of the Jews had fallen upon them.

יז וּבְכָל־מְדִינָה וּמְדִינָה וּבְכָל־עִיר וָעִיר מְקוֹם אֲשֶׁר דְּבַר־הַמֶּלֶךְ וְדָתוֹ מַגִּיעַ שִׂמְחָה וְשָׂשׂוֹן לַיְּהוּדִים מִשְׁתֶּה וְיוֹם טוֹב וְרַבִּים מֵעַמֵּי הָאָרֶץ מִתְיַהֲדִים כִּי־נָפַל פַּחַד־הַיְּהוּדִים עֲלֵיהֶם:

uv-KHOL m'-dee-NAH um-dee-NAH uv-KHOL EER va-EER m'-KOM a-SHER d'-VAR ha-ME-lekh v'-da-TO ma-GEE-a sim-KHAH v'-sa-SON la-y'-hu-DEEM mish-TEH v'-YOM TOV v'-ra-BEEM may-a-MAY ha-A-retz mit-ya-ha-DEEM KEE na-FAL PA-khad ha-y'-hu-DEEM a-lay-HEM

which precedes the High Holidays, is conducive to repentance. *Av*, the month in which the two Temples in Jerusalem were destroyed, is a month of mourning, and *Nisan*, the month in which the exodus from Egypt occurred, is the same month in which the ultimate redemption will take place in the future. The joyous holiday of *Purim* is celebrated in the month of *Adar*, and the Sages tell us that "when *Adar* comes, joy increases" (*Ta'anit* 29a). Each season has its own unique energy, and one can more easily tap into those qualities during the corresponding times of year. *Adar* is the time when we can most easily access feelings of happiness and joy.

8:17 Came close to the Jews What exactly did the non-Jews at the time do? In Hebrew, the word is *"Mityahadim,"* which is an unusual word as this is the only place in the entire *Tanakh* in which this word appears. The King James Bible translates this as "became Jews", to imply that many Persians converted to Judaism at that time. Many Jewish scholars disagree, since Judaism discourages proselytizing, and interpret it as referring to many who "came close" to the Jewish people. *Rabbenu Bachye* and the *Sfat Emet* explain that just like non-Jews came close to the Jewish people at the time of the *Purim* story, so too in the future, the nations of the world will turn toward the Jews in admiration and friendship. This verse serves as a dramatic capstone to the original miracle, where the very enemies who tried to kill us became our allies at the end of the story. We pray for the day when all those still trying to harm the Jewish people put down their weapons and turn towards Israel in peace.

CHAPTER 9
פרק ט

CHAPTER 9

ON THE 13TH OF *ADAR*, THE DAY ON WHICH THE JEWISH people were supposed to be annihilated, the tables are turned and the Jews gather to defend themselves. In many provinces they are unopposed. In Shushan, the Jews kill Haman's ten sons, as well as five hundred other enemies. As the numbers arrive at the palace, Ahasuerus offers to grant *Esther* another request. *Esther* asks that the Jews in Shushan be allowed to defend themselves for another day, on the 14th of *Adar*. Mordechai establishes the 14th and 15th of *Adar* as annual celebrations of feasting and merrymaking as well as sending gifts to one another and presents to the poor. These days are called "*Purim*," because of the lottery, or *pur*, which Haman drew. The Jews accept these days upon themselves for all generations.

1 In the twelfth month, which is the month of *Adar*, on its thirteenth day, wherever the king's command and decree had reached and were to be executed, on the day that the eneimes of the Jews thought that they would overcome them, it was the opposite, in that the Jews overcame their enemies.

א וּבִשְׁנֵים עָשָׂר חֹדֶשׁ הוּא־חֹדֶשׁ אֲדָר בִּשְׁלוֹשָׁה עָשָׂר יוֹם בּוֹ אֲשֶׁר הִגִּיעַ דְּבַר־הַמֶּלֶךְ וְדָתוֹ לְהֵעָשׂוֹת בַּיּוֹם אֲשֶׁר שִׂבְּרוּ אֹיְבֵי הַיְּהוּדִים לִשְׁלוֹט בָּהֶם וְנַהֲפוֹךְ הוּא אֲשֶׁר יִשְׁלְטוּ הַיְּהוּדִים הֵמָּה בְּשֹׂנְאֵיהֶם:

2 The Jews assembled in their cities in every province of King Ahasuerus to raise their hand against those who sought to harm them. No man could stand before them, for fear of them had befallen all of the people.

ב נִקְהֲלוּ הַיְּהוּדִים בְּעָרֵיהֶם בְּכָל־מְדִינוֹת הַמֶּלֶךְ אֲחַשְׁוֵרוֹשׁ לִשְׁלֹחַ יָד בִּמְבַקְשֵׁי רָעָתָם וְאִישׁ לֹא־עָמַד לִפְנֵיהֶם כִּי־נָפַל פַּחְדָּם עַל־כָּל־הָעַמִּים:

Esther
CHAPTER 9

3 Every minister of the provinces, regional governor, provincial governor, and those who do the king's work exalted the Jews since the trepidation of *Mordechai* fell upon them.

4 For *Mordechai* was prominent in the royal palace, and his fame spread through all the provinces since *Mordechai* became increasingly great.

5 The Jews struck down all their enemies with the sword, slaying, and destroying them. They did to their enemies as they wished.

6 In the capital of Shushan, the Jews slew five hundred men.

7 Along with Parshandatha, Dalphon, Aspatha,

8 Poratha, Adalia, Aridatha,

9 Parmashta, Arisai, Aridai, and Vaizatha,

10 ten sons of Haman, the son of Hammedatha, the enemy of the Jews. But, they did not touch the spoils.

11 On that day the number of those killed in the capital of Shushan came before the king.

אסתר · פרק ט

ג וְכָל־שָׂרֵי הַמְּדִינוֹת וְהָאֲחַשְׁדַּרְפְּנִים וְהַפַּחוֹת וְעֹשֵׂי הַמְּלָאכָה אֲשֶׁר לַמֶּלֶךְ מְנַשְּׂאִים אֶת־הַיְּהוּדִים כִּי־נָפַל פַּחַד־מָרְדֳּכַי עֲלֵיהֶם:

ד כִּי־גָדוֹל מָרְדֳּכַי בְּבֵית הַמֶּלֶךְ וְשָׁמְעוֹ הוֹלֵךְ בְּכָל־הַמְּדִינוֹת כִּי־הָאִישׁ מָרְדֳּכַי הוֹלֵךְ וְגָדוֹל:

ה וַיַּכּוּ הַיְּהוּדִים בְּכָל־אֹיְבֵיהֶם מַכַּת־חֶרֶב וְהֶרֶג וְאַבְדָן וַיַּעֲשׂוּ בְשֹׂנְאֵיהֶם כִּרְצוֹנָם:

ו וּבְשׁוּשַׁן הַבִּירָה הָרְגוּ הַיְּהוּדִים וְאַבֵּד חֲמֵשׁ מֵאוֹת אִישׁ:

ז וְאֵת פַּרְשַׁנְדָּתָא וְאֵת דַּלְפוֹן וְאֵת אַסְפָּתָא:

ח וְאֵת פּוֹרָתָא וְאֵת אֲדַלְיָא וְאֵת אֲרִידָתָא:

ט וְאֵת פַּרְמַשְׁתָּא וְאֵת אֲרִיסַי וְאֵת אֲרִדַי וְאֵת וַיְזָתָא:

י עֲשֶׂרֶת בְּנֵי הָמָן בֶּן־הַמְּדָתָא צֹרֵר הַיְּהוּדִים הָרָגוּ וּבַבִּזָּה לֹא שָׁלְחוּ אֶת־יָדָם:

יא בַּיּוֹם הַהוּא בָּא מִסְפַּר הַהֲרוּגִים בְּשׁוּשַׁן הַבִּירָה לִפְנֵי הַמֶּלֶךְ:

61 · *Esther*
CHAPTER 9

12 The king said to Queen *Esther*, "In the capital of Shushan the Jews killed and destroyed five hundred men and ten sons of Haman. Likewise have they done in the other provinces of the king. What is your wish? It will be granted to you. What is your request? It shall be done."

13 *Esther* replied, "If it pleases the king, allow the Jews in Shushan tomorrow also to fulfill the decree as they did today, and hang the ten sons of Haman on the gallows."

14 The king said that this should be done, and the decree went out in Shushan. The ten sons of Haman were hanged.

15 The Jews in Shushan assembled also on the fourteenth of the month of *Adar* and slew three hundred men in Shushan, but they did not touch the spoils.

16 The rest of the Jews that were in the provinces of the king gathered and defended themselves. They had respite from their enemies, having slayed seventy-five thousand of their adversaries, but they did not touch the spoils.

אסתר
פרק ט

יב וַיֹּאמֶר הַמֶּלֶךְ לְאֶסְתֵּר הַמַּלְכָּה בְּשׁוּשַׁן הַבִּירָה הָרְגוּ הַיְּהוּדִים וְאַבֵּד חֲמֵשׁ מֵאוֹת אִישׁ וְאֵת עֲשֶׂרֶת בְּנֵי־הָמָן בִּשְׁאָר מְדִינוֹת הַמֶּלֶךְ מֶה עָשׂוּ וּמַה־שְּׁאֵלָתֵךְ וְיִנָּתֵן לָךְ וּמַה־בַּקָּשָׁתֵךְ עוֹד וְתֵעָשׂ׃

יג וַתֹּאמֶר אֶסְתֵּר אִם־עַל־הַמֶּלֶךְ טוֹב יִנָּתֵן גַּם־מָחָר לַיְּהוּדִים אֲשֶׁר בְּשׁוּשָׁן לַעֲשׂוֹת כְּדָת הַיּוֹם וְאֵת עֲשֶׂרֶת בְּנֵי־הָמָן יִתְלוּ עַל־הָעֵץ׃

יד וַיֹּאמֶר הַמֶּלֶךְ לְהֵעָשׂוֹת כֵּן וַתִּנָּתֵן דָּת בְּשׁוּשָׁן וְאֵת עֲשֶׂרֶת בְּנֵי־הָמָן תָּלוּ׃

טו וַיִּקָּהֲלוּ היהודיים [הַיְּהוּדִים] אֲשֶׁר־בְּשׁוּשָׁן גַּם בְּיוֹם אַרְבָּעָה עָשָׂר לְחֹדֶשׁ אֲדָר וַיַּהַרְגוּ בְשׁוּשָׁן שְׁלֹשׁ מֵאוֹת אִישׁ וּבַבִּזָּה לֹא שָׁלְחוּ אֶת־יָדָם׃

טז וּשְׁאָר הַיְּהוּדִים אֲשֶׁר בִּמְדִינוֹת הַמֶּלֶךְ נִקְהֲלוּ וְעָמֹד עַל־נַפְשָׁם וְנוֹחַ מֵאֹיְבֵיהֶם וְהָרֹג בְּשֹׂנְאֵיהֶם חֲמִשָּׁה וְשִׁבְעִים אָלֶף וּבַבִּזָּה לֹא שָׁלְחוּ אֶת־יָדָם׃

Esther
CHAPTER 9

17 They fought on the thirteenth day of the month of *Adar,* and rested on the fourteenth day, which they made into a day of feasting and celebration.

יז בְּיוֹם־שְׁלֹשָׁה עָשָׂר לְחֹדֶשׁ אֲדָר וְנוֹחַ בְּאַרְבָּעָה עָשָׂר בּוֹ וְעָשֹׂה אֹתוֹ יוֹם מִשְׁתֶּה וְשִׂמְחָה:

b'-YOM sh'-lo-SHAH a-SAR l-KHO-desh a-DAR v'-NO-akh b'-ar-ba-AH a-SAR BO v'-a-SOH o-TO yom mish-TEH v'-sim-KHAH

18 The Jews in Shushan assembled on the thirteenth and the fourteenth, and rested on the fifteenth. They made it into a day of feasting and celebration.

יח וְהַיְּהוּדִיים [וְהַיְּהוּדִים] אֲשֶׁר־בְּשׁוּשָׁן נִקְהֲלוּ בִּשְׁלֹשָׁה עָשָׂר בּוֹ וּבְאַרְבָּעָה עָשָׂר בּוֹ וְנוֹחַ בַּחֲמִשָּׁה עָשָׂר בּוֹ וְעָשֹׂה אֹתוֹ יוֹם מִשְׁתֶּה וְשִׂמְחָה:

9:17 Day of feasting and celebration
The Hebrew word for celebration in this verse is *simcha* (שמחה) which, according to Rabbi Mordechai Willig, refers to an exuberant but temporary experience of joy felt on special occasions. There is, however, another kind of happiness: *sasson* (ששון). Rabbi Willig explains that *sasson* is the enduring happy feeling of satisfaction and fulfillment. The feeling of *simcha* is more intense but short lived, while *sasson* is less powerful but persists endlessly. When describing *Yerushalayim* in the end of days, at the time of redemption, *Yirmiyahu* uses both of these terms: "Again there shall be heard in this place… the sound of joy (*sasson*) and celebration (*simcha*)" (Jeremiah 33:10–11). *Yirmiyahu* promises that one day the Land of Israel will be filled with the sweet sounds of both *sasson* and *simcha*. Not only will there be exuberant joy over the redemption, but the people will experience the long-lasting satisfaction of dwelling permanently in *Eretz Yisrael* in the presence of *Hashem*.

63 · *Esther*

CHAPTER 9

אסתר
פרק ט

19 Therefore, the Jews who are villagers and live in open villages celebrate on the fourteenth day of the month of *Adar* with happiness, feasting, and a holiday sending portions of food to each other.

יט עַל־כֵּן הַיְּהוּדִים הַפְּרָזִים [הַפְּרָזִים] הַיֹּשְׁבִים בְּעָרֵי הַפְּרָזוֹת עֹשִׂים אֵת יוֹם אַרְבָּעָה עָשָׂר לְחֹדֶשׁ אֲדָר שִׂמְחָה וּמִשְׁתֶּה וְיוֹם טוֹב וּמִשְׁלוֹחַ מָנוֹת אִישׁ לְרֵעֵהוּ׃

al KAYN ha-y'-hu-DEEM ha-p'-ra-ZEEM ha-yo-sh'-VEEM b'-a-RAY ha-p'-ra-ZOT o-SEEM AYT YOM ar-ba-AH a-SAR l'-KHO-desh a-DAR sim-KHAH u-mish-TEH v'-YOM TOV u-mish-LO-akh ma-NOT EESH l'-ray-AY-hu

20 *Mordechai* recorded these matters, and sent scrolls to all of the Jews in every province of King Ahasuerus, near and far.

כ וַיִּכְתֹּב מָרְדֳּכַי אֶת־הַדְּבָרִים הָאֵלֶּה וַיִּשְׁלַח סְפָרִים אֶל־כָּל־הַיְּהוּדִים אֲשֶׁר בְּכָל־מְדִינוֹת הַמֶּלֶךְ אֲחַשְׁוֵרוֹשׁ הַקְּרוֹבִים וְהָרְחוֹקִים׃

9:19 Sending portions of food to each other The Jews in Shushan united and came together when *Esther* called them to fast, and so *Purim* is observed with four specific commandments (*mitzvot*), all of which demonstrate unity and brotherly love. The first commandment involves the public reading of *Megillat Esther* for one and all, old and young. A second commandment requires individuals to pack festive food packages and deliver them to friends or the needy as described in our verse. A third commandment mandates that charity be given to the poor. The Sages even states that on *Purim* we are to give charity to "all who extend a hand" without scrutiny or asking any questions. Finally, there is a commandment to have a lavish holiday meal, shared with many others. *Purim* underscores just how much of a difference we can make when we love and care for one another.

Esther
CHAPTER 9

64 אסתר · פרק ט

21 To obligate them to establish the fourteenth day of the month of *Adar* and the fifteenth day each and every year

כא לְקַיֵּם עֲלֵיהֶם לִהְיוֹת עֹשִׂים אֵת יוֹם אַרְבָּעָה עָשָׂר לְחֹדֶשׁ אֲדָר וְאֵת יוֹם־חֲמִשָּׁה עָשָׂר בּוֹ בְּכָל־שָׁנָה וְשָׁנָה:

l'-ka-YAYM a-lay-HEM lih-YOT o-SEEM AYT YOM ar-ba-AH a-SAR l'-KHO-desh a-DAR v'-AYT yom kha-mi-SHAH a-SAR BO b'-khol sha-NAH v'-sha-NAH

22 like the days that the Jews rested from their enemies and the month that had turned from sadness to happiness and from mourning to holiday. They should make these to be days of feasting and happiness, along with sending portions of food to one another and giving gifts to the poor.

כב כַּיָּמִים אֲשֶׁר־נָחוּ בָהֶם הַיְּהוּדִים מֵאוֹיְבֵיהֶם וְהַחֹדֶשׁ אֲשֶׁר נֶהְפַּךְ לָהֶם מִיָּגוֹן לְשִׂמְחָה וּמֵאֵבֶל לְיוֹם טוֹב לַעֲשׂוֹת אוֹתָם יְמֵי מִשְׁתֶּה וְשִׂמְחָה וּמִשְׁלוֹחַ מָנוֹת אִישׁ לְרֵעֵהוּ וּמַתָּנוֹת לָאֶבְיוֹנִים:

ka-ya-MEEM a-sher NA-khu va-HEM ha-y'-hu-DEEM may-o-y'-vay-HEM v'-ha-KHO-desh a-SHER neh-PAKH la-HEM mi-ya-GON l'-sim-KHAH u-may-AY-vel l'-YOM TOV la-a-SOT o-TAM y'-MAY mish-TEH v'-sim-KHAH u-mish-LO-akh ma-NOT EESH l'-ray-AY-hu u-ma-ta-NOT la-ev-yo-NEEM

9:21 The fourteenth and fifteenth *Purim* is the only Jewish holiday that is observed on two different days, depending on one's location. The residents of cities with walls around them, like *Yerushalayim*, celebrate on the fifteenth of *Adar*, while the rest of the world celebrates on the fourteenth. In establishing the holiday of *Purim*, *Esther* wanted to guarantee that the lesson of *Purim* would not be forgotten. In her time, the Children of Israel had forsaken Jerusalem when they feasted at a party celebrating its destruction. Observing *Purim* in *Yerushalayim* on a different day highlights its special status and its eternal connection to the People of Israel.

9:22 Rested from their enemies Today in Israel, when a terror attack occur, it is not uncommon for Arabs to celebrate

65 · Esther
CHAPTER 9

אסתר
פרק ט

23 The Jews accepted to maintain that which they began to do and that which *Mordechai* wrote to them.

כג וְקִבֵּל הַיְּהוּדִים אֵת אֲשֶׁר־הֵחֵלּוּ לַעֲשׂוֹת וְאֵת אֲשֶׁר־כָּתַב מָרְדֳּכַי אֲלֵיהֶם:

24 For, Haman, the son of Hammedatha the Agagite, who was the enemy of all the Jews, plotted to annihilate the Jews. He drew a *pur*, which is a lot, to cause them to panic and to destroy them.

כד כִּי הָמָן בֶּן־הַמְּדָתָא הָאֲגָגִי צֹרֵר כָּל־הַיְּהוּדִים חָשַׁב עַל־הַיְּהוּדִים לְאַבְּדָם וְהִפִּיל פּוּר הוּא הַגּוֹרָל לְהֻמָּם וּלְאַבְּדָם:

25 When she came before the king, he declared through sending scrolls that Haman's evil plan, which he devised against the Jews, should turn upon its head. They, subsequently, hanged him and his sons on the gallows.

כה וּבְבֹאָהּ לִפְנֵי הַמֶּלֶךְ אָמַר עִם־הַסֵּפֶר יָשׁוּב מַחֲשַׁבְתּוֹ הָרָעָה אֲשֶׁר־חָשַׁב עַל־הַיְּהוּדִים עַל־רֹאשׁוֹ וְתָלוּ אֹתוֹ וְאֶת־בָּנָיו עַל־הָעֵץ:

26 Therefore, they called these days *Purim* after the lottery. Due to all that was written in this letter and because of what they saw regarding this and what transpired to them,

כו עַל־כֵּן קָרְאוּ לַיָּמִים הָאֵלֶּה פוּרִים עַל־שֵׁם הַפּוּר עַל־כֵּן עַל־כָּל־דִּבְרֵי הָאִגֶּרֶת הַזֹּאת וּמָה־רָאוּ עַל־כָּכָה וּמָה הִגִּיעַ אֲלֵיהֶם:

27 the Jews affirmed and accepted upon themselves, their descendants, and all those who join them to mark these two days as they are written and according to their times each and every year.

כז קִיְּמוּ וְקִבֵּל [וְקִבְּלוּ] הַיְּהוּדִים עֲלֵיהֶם וְעַל־זַרְעָם וְעַל כָּל־הַנִּלְוִים עֲלֵיהֶם וְלֹא יַעֲבוֹר לִהְיוֹת עֹשִׂים אֵת שְׁנֵי הַיָּמִים הָאֵלֶּה כִּכְתָבָם וְכִזְמַנָּם בְּכָל־שָׁנָה וְשָׁנָה:

Purim and their salvation in the time of Ahasuerus, the date of the holiday is not the day they won the war, but rather the day after, when they rested from their enemies. The focus of the celebration is not the fall of the enemy, but the relief that comes in its wake.

the carnage by handing out candy in the streets. The *Torah*, however, emphasizes universal feelings of sympathy and compassion for all, and warns against rejoicing at the downfall of our enemies (Proverbs 24:17). For this reason, when the Jewish people annually celebrate

Esther
CHAPTER 9

28 These days should be memorialized and commemorated in each and every generation, by each and every family in each and every province, and in each and every city. These days of *Purim* will never be omitted by the Jews, neither will the memory be abandoned by their descendants.

29 Queen *Esther bat Avichayil*, and *Mordechai* the Jew then wrote a letter with full authority to reinforce this second letter regarding *Purim*.

30 Scrolls were sent to all the Jews in the one hundred and twenty-seven provinces of Ahasuerus's kingdom bearing a message of peace and truth.

31 To uphold these days of *Purim* in their proper times as *Mordechai* the Jew and *Esther* the queen established the fasting and the crying out for them and for their descendants.

32 The decree of *Esther* established these matters of *Purim*, and it was recorded in a scroll.

אסתר • 66
פרק ט

כח וְהַיָּמִים הָאֵלֶּה נִזְכָּרִים וְנַעֲשִׂים בְּכׇל־דּוֹר וָדוֹר מִשְׁפָּחָה וּמִשְׁפָּחָה מְדִינָה וּמְדִינָה וְעִיר וָעִיר וִימֵי הַפּוּרִים הָאֵלֶּה לֹא יַעַבְרוּ מִתּוֹךְ הַיְּהוּדִים וְזִכְרָם לֹא־יָסוּף מִזַּרְעָם׃

כט וַתִּכְתֹּב אֶסְתֵּר הַמַּלְכָּה בַת־אֲבִיחַיִל וּמׇרְדֳּכַי הַיְּהוּדִי אֶת־כׇּל־תֹּקֶף לְקַיֵּם אֵת אִגֶּרֶת הַפֻּרִים הַזֹּאת הַשֵּׁנִית׃

ל וַיִּשְׁלַח סְפָרִים אֶל־כׇּל־הַיְּהוּדִים אֶל־שֶׁבַע וְעֶשְׂרִים וּמֵאָה מְדִינָה מַלְכוּת אֲחַשְׁוֵרוֹשׁ דִּבְרֵי שָׁלוֹם וֶאֱמֶת׃

לא לְקַיֵּם אֶת־יְמֵי הַפֻּרִים הָאֵלֶּה בִּזְמַנֵּיהֶם כַּאֲשֶׁר קִיַּם עֲלֵיהֶם מׇרְדֳּכַי הַיְּהוּדִי וְאֶסְתֵּר הַמַּלְכָּה וְכַאֲשֶׁר קִיְּמוּ עַל־נַפְשָׁם וְעַל־זַרְעָם דִּבְרֵי הַצּוֹמוֹת וְזַעֲקָתָם׃

לב וּמַאֲמַר אֶסְתֵּר קִיַּם דִּבְרֵי הַפֻּרִים הָאֵלֶּה וְנִכְתָּב בַּסֵּפֶר׃

CHAPTER 10
פרק י

CHAPTER 10

AFTER THE *PURIM* STORY IS COMPLETE, AHASUERUS enacts a new tax and the story of *Mordechai*'s rise to power and greatness is written in the royal Persian records. *Mordechai* is now second to Ahasuerus and finds favor in the eyes of most of his brethren. He seeks the good of his people and peace for all generations.

1 And King Ahasuerus placed a tax upon the land and upon the sea islands.

2 All of his strength and might, along with the ascension of *Mordechai* who the king exalted, are recorded in the scroll of archives of the kings of Media and Persia.

א וַיָּשֶׂם הַמֶּלֶךְ אחשרש [אֲחַשְׁוֵרוֹשׁ] מַס עַל־הָאָרֶץ וְאִיֵּי הַיָּם:

ב וְכָל־מַעֲשֵׂה תָקְפּוֹ וּגְבוּרָתוֹ וּפָרָשַׁת גְּדֻלַּת מָרְדֳּכַי אֲשֶׁר גִּדְּלוֹ הַמֶּלֶךְ הֲלוֹא־הֵם כְּתוּבִים עַל־סֵפֶר דִּבְרֵי הַיָּמִים לְמַלְכֵי מָדַי וּפָרָס:

Esther
CHAPTER 10

70 · אסתר
פרק י

3 For *Mordechai* the Jew was second to King Ahasuerus and was a leader among the Jews. He was appreciated by the majority of his brethren, he sought to benefit his nation and was a spokesman of peace for all his descendants.

ג כִּי מָרְדֳּכַי הַיְּהוּדִי מִשְׁנֶה לַמֶּלֶךְ אֲחַשְׁוֵרוֹשׁ וְגָדוֹל לַיְּהוּדִים וְרָצוּי לְרֹב אֶחָיו דֹּרֵשׁ טוֹב לְעַמּוֹ וְדֹבֵר שָׁלוֹם לְכָל־זַרְעוֹ:

KEE mor-d'-KHAI ha-y'-hu-DEE mish-NEH la-ME-lekh a-khash-vay-ROSH v'-ga-DOL la-y'-hu-DEEM v'-ra-TZUY l'-ROV e-KHAV do-RAYSH TOV l'-a-MO v'-do-VAYR sha-LOM l'-khol zar-O

10:3 For *Mordechai* the Jew was second to King Ahasuerus According to one opinion among the Sages, this verse describes two stages of *Mordechai's* life following the *Purim* story. Initially, he was "second to King Ahasuerus" until Darius, son of *Esther* and Ahasuerus, allowed the rebuilding of the *Beit Hamikdash*. At that point, according to Jewish tradition, *Mordechai* stepped down from his exalted governmental position to return to Israel where he was responsible for the offerings in the *Beit Hamikdash* (see *Mishna Shekalim* 5:1). Dismissing the glory he achieved in the palace of Ahasuerus, *Mordechai* then became "appreciated by his brethren." He did not let honor and fame stand in the way of his values, and in a fitting conclusion to *Megillat Esther*, *Mordechai* returns to the Land of Israel and takes an active role in the service of the Second *Beit Hamikdash*. Mordechai thus serves as not only the leader of his generation, but as an inspiring example for our generation as well. After 2,000 years of exile, the Jewish People should set aside their positions, no matter how comfortable or prestigious they may be, and return to the Land of Israel. If more Jews follow the example of *Mordechai*, we will surely merit to soon begin building the Third *Beit Hamikdash in Yerushalayim*.

FEAR

Esther Horgen

Esther Horgen wrote this poem in 2015, following a particularly brutal month when a boy was stabbed just weeks before his Bar Mitzvah.

Translated from French by Benjamin Horgen and Lauren Gordon

Last photo taken of Esther Horgen walking through the forest

    For some people, the purpose of terror attacks is to awaken or
        to punish us.
    For others, God has lost control of the situation.
    Many others feel invaded by terror.
    What hides behind these fears?

    These fears were already present,
    terrorism merely externalized them.

We become aware of our fears,
able to understand them and to draw personal conclusions.
We know how to overcome fear of dying,
after all, we drive in our cars every day.
Where does this fear that has crept
into so many of our hearts come from?

Fear reflects our lack of faith in ourselves, in life, in God.
Even the knowledge that absolutely everything
is under Hashem's perfect control,
and that there is never any loss of divine control,
does not always soothe a troubled heart.

Terrorism is the result of a fanatical idea taken to the extreme.
Divine devotion, a lofty ideal,
is turned inside-out like a glove and filled with blasphemies.
Divine love and patience become inhuman hatred and violence.
If terrorism, then, imposes its hatred and violence on humanity,
let us offer love and kindness.

I am not responsible for the thoughts and feelings of others,
only for my own,
so I seek to make the changes that are within my power –
in my heart, my thoughts, my deeds and my words.

What if terrorism was the explosion of mankind's accumulated
    mental violence?
By mental violence,
I mean truths that we are taught but do not bother to verify or
    develop.
By mental violence,
I mean truths that I impose on others, without love or kindness.
By mental violence,
I mean critical thoughts about yourself, others and the situation.

By this violence,
I mean the attitude of constantly placing yourself in second place,
below your spouse, children, or career.

Violence always begins with ourselves.
We harm ourselves by listening to the voices of fear, doubt, lack
 of faith.
We ignore that behind these voices hide the wonderful force
 of life
which continues to blossom.
Joy, altruism and faith that light is more powerful than darkness,
that love wins over hatred and that joy overcomes mourning.

All truth must be questioned, reworked and then revitalized,
otherwise it becomes fanaticism.
Personally, I hold no absolute truths in the world of ideas.
Of course, I hold many truths in my heart;
not what I have been taught, but what I feel.
My subjective truths are those that resonate within me,
like the love of my family or my people, like the desire for peace,
 joy and unity.

Of course, God is Truth, the greatest of my certainties,
but if someone asks me to prove His existence,
I have no rational words to do so, since as love cannot be ex-
 plained,
neither can the certainty of God.

Mental patience is choosing to remain innocent,
because something bigger than us is pulling the strings.
Mental patience is listening to my fellow human (if he is human!)
with a heart open to the intrinsic good within him.
This kindness of spirit, of course, begins with oneself.

Listen to yourself, respect yourself, please yourself and be filled
  with calm.
Feel deeply that we are always – yes, always – under His protection.

And whenever a situation reminds me of my helplessness,
like seeing a child stabbed a month before his Bar Mitzvah,
our prayers join with his mother's prayers,
crossing hearts beyond the oceans,
imploring the Divine Mercy that lies dormant within us.

It is from the depths of our helplessness that we encounter
  Omnipotence.
You have to live it to understand it.

LA PEUR
Esther Horgen

POUR LES UNS LES ATTENTATS ONT POUR RÔLE DE RÉVEILLER, ou de punir, pour d'autres Di-eu a perdu le contrôle de la situation. Pour beaucoup la terreur les a envahis… Que cachent ces peurs ? Certes leur existence précède le terrorisme, celui-ci les extériorise, permettant d'en prendre conscience, de les comprendre, et d'en tirer les conséquences personnelles. Nous savons surmonter la peur de mourir puisque nous voyageons en voiture. Et cette peur qui aujourd'hui s'est insinuée dans tant de cœurs, d'où vient-elle ? Les peurs reflètent notre manque de confiance, en soi, en la vie, en Hachem. La connaissance que Tout absolument Tout est sous le contrôle parfait d'Hachem, qu'il n'y a aucun dérapage divin, n'apaise pas toujours les cœurs agités.

Le terrorisme est la résultante d'une idée fanatique, poussée à l'extrême. Une idée a priori belle et élevée, la dévotion divine, retournée

comme un gant, en plus grand des blasphèmes. Amour et patience divines se retournent en haine et violence inhumaines. Si le terrorisme impose à l'humanité sa haine et sa violence, offrons-nous amour et douceur. Je ne suis responsable ni des ressentis ni des pensées des autres, mais des miennes, donc je recherche des améliorations là où j'ai du pouvoir. Au sein de mon cœur de mes pensées actes et paroles.

Et si le terrorisme était l'explosion de l'accumulation des violences mentales de l'humanité. J'entends par violence mentale des vérités que l'on nous enseigne, et que nous ne prenons pas la peine de vérifier, ni de les faire évoluer. J'entends par violences mentales des vérités que j'impose aux autres, sans amour ni douceur. J'entends par violences mentales les pensées critiques, de soi, de l'autre et de la situation. J'entends par ces violences l'attitude de se mettre systématiquement en seconde priorité, après le conjoint, les enfants, la carrière. La violence commence toujours par soi-même, se faire violence c'est écouter les voix de la peur, du doute, de la non-confiance omettant que derrière elles se cachent la force merveilleuse de la vie qui continue à éclore, la joie, l'altruisme, la Emouna que la lumière est plus puissante que l'obscurité, que l'amour remporte sur la haine, la joie sur le deuil.

Toute vérité doit être remise en question, remaniée et revitalisée, sinon elle devient du fanatisme. Personnellement, je n'ai aucune vérité absolue dans le monde des idées, j'en ai bien sûr beaucoup dans mon cœur, non celles que l'on ma enseignées, mais celle que je ressens. Mes vérités subjectives, celles qui vibrent en moi, comme l'Amour de ma famille ou de mon peuple, comme le désir de paix de joie et d'unité etc. Bien sûr, Di-eu est une Vérité, la plus grande de mes certitudes, mais si quelqu'un me demande de lui prouver son existence, je n'aurai aucun mot rationnel pour le lui prouver, puisque comme l'amour ne s'explique pas, la certitude de Di-eu encore moins.

La patience mentale, c'est choisir de rester dans la naïveté innocente, parce que plus grand que soi tire les ficelles du spectacle. La patience mentale c'est écouter mon prochain (s'il est humain !!!) avec le cœur

ouvert à l'intrinsèquement bon qui l'habite. Cette douceur de l'esprit commence bien sûr par soi-même. S'écouter, se respecter, se faire plaisir et s'apaiser. Sentir profondément que nous sommes toujours, oui toujours sous Sa protection. Et chaque fois qu'une situation me rappelle mon impuissance, comme de voir un enfant poignardé un mois avant sa Bar Mitsva, nos prières se joignent à la prière de sa mère, traversant les cœurs au-delà des océans, implorant la Miséricorde divine, endormie en nous. C'est du plus profond de notre impuissance, que nous rencontrons la Toute-puissance. Il faut le vivre pour le comprendre.

QUEEN ESTHER. CHANA SENESH. ANNE FRANK. ESTHER HORGEN

Rabbi Tuly Weisz

Esther Horgen, with her arms outstretched, embracing the world

LIKE QUEEN ESTHER, CHANA SENESH OR ANNE FRANK, ESTHER Horgen is that once-in-a-generation Jewish heroine, whose true greatness is only widely recognized from her writings following her death.

I did not know Esther personally, but was moved to organize a crowdfunding campaign showing support for her family after hearing the news of her tragic murder thirty days ago. As a stranger walking nervously into the shiva home limited by Corona restrictions, I found myself warmly welcomed by Esther's husband Benjamin. The first thing he told me was that for Esther, there were no strangers, only old friends and new ones. Benjamin then expressed to me how grateful he felt to the nearly 1,000 new friends who conveyed their condolences and sympathies to his family.

Many of the donations came from Jews who learned of the effort on social media from *Jerusalem Post* columnist Hillel Fuld and through an article that appeared in this newspaper. Other contributions came from Christian Zionists through Israel365, and so I told Benjamin that hundreds of Jews and Christians from all over the world are crying with you today.

Benjamin pointed to that week's Torah portion about Joseph weeping on the neck of his brother Benjamin and assured me that he too felt the embrace, the tears and the love from his brothers and sisters. Benjamin then shared with me a remarkable article that Esther wrote after telling me all about his special wife.

Esther was a vivacious woman who loved life and lived every moment to its fullest. Family photos scattered throughout the Horgen home captured her in most pictures with arms open wide, embracing her world with youthful enthusiasm that belied her 52 years. A mother of six and grandmother to two babies, Esther was an artist who studied Jewish psychology and loved to exercise in nature.

Born in France, Esther first came to visit Israel with her parents as a young girl and fell in love with the idealism, romanticism and spiritual energy of the Jewish State. Before returning to Paris, the 10-year-old told her mother and father, "Israel is my home and I will be moving there one day."

While still a teenager, Esther made Aliyah and met and married Benjamin, another French immigrant. They settled in a town in Samaria called *Tal Menashe* (the dew of Menasseh), in the territory of Menasseh, that took its name from a Biblical miracle that occurred there involving dew.

On a sunny, Sunday afternoon, Esther laced up her sneakers for a jog in the scenic forest just outside her home. There, in her beloved nature reserve, Esther was brutally murdered by Muhammed Marwah Kabha from the nearby Palestinian town of Jenin, who was lying in ambush waiting for a victim. Muhammed smashed Esther's head repeatedly with

a rock, which he later confessed was revenge for the death of a terrorist who died of cancer while in Israeli custody.

Esther's murder was the result of the Palestinian Authority's ongoing demonization of Israel for its alleged mistreatment of hospitalized criminals. These lies are picked up routinely and repeated around the world. Therefore, to many governments and media outlets, Esther was just another "settler" who "occupied illegal territory."

Labels have implications and words lead to actions, which in Esther's case had deadly consequences.

Anyone who sees photos of Esther can tell this woman was no criminal. However, as a resident of Judea and Samaria confronted with violence on a constant basis, one might have expected Esther to have developed a hardened outlook in response to the constant threat of terror. Esther did in fact think deeply about life and death, violence and evil. Following a particularly brutal month in 2015 when a boy was stabbed weeks before his Bar Mitzvah, she wrote an essay she titled "Fear."

Esther's words have hallowed significance for our generation:

> "Terrorism is the result of a fanatical idea taken to the extreme. A beautiful idea of devotion to the Divine is turned inside out like a glove into inhuman hatred and violence. But if terrorism imposes its hatred and violence on humanity, let us respond with love and gentleness.
>
> "I have no control over the thoughts and feelings of others, so I must seek to improve what I can control. That which is within my heart, my thoughts, my deeds and my words... Light is more powerful than darkness, love wins over hatred, joy overcomes mourning.
>
> "...Whenever a situation reminds me of my helplessness, like seeing a child stabbed a month before his Bar Mitzvah, our prayers join with his mother's prayers, crossing hearts beyond the oceans, imploring the Divine Mercy that lies dormant within us. It is from the depths of our helplessness that we encounter Omnipotence. You have to live it to understand it."

Esther's poem echo the Hebrew prophets, containing the wisdom of Proverbs and the poetry of Psalms. While they are contemporary, they are not superficial. That she paid the ultimate price for her beliefs requires us to internalize them deeply.

On a daily basis, I teach Christians about Israel and Torah from a Jewish perspective. I have the unique honor of sharing Judaic wisdom from our greatest ancient philosophers to our brilliant modern sages. Yet, through her life, her death and her words, Esther Horgen taught me more about Biblical values and Jewish ideals than any Torah scholar.

The role of the Jewish people has always been to be a kingdom of priests and holy nation. We were the first to introduce morality and values to the world, encapsulated by our mandate to be a light unto the nations. This noble mission has always been the source of both admiration and hostility. Throughout our history, our enemies have rejected what the Jewish people stand for and accused us of all kinds of terrible offenses, similar to the crimes with which Muhammed Marwah Kabha demonized Esther Horgen.

Esther's murder is not an isolated incident or an unexpected bump on an otherwise peaceful road in the resettlement of the People of Israel in the Land of Israel. Our world desperately needs to strain its ear to listen to a still, small voice in the wilderness, or look towards a shining light to illuminate the darkness all around us.

Esther Horgen is that voice and that light for our generation, and by internalizing her words, we can keep her memory alive, so that her death is not in vain.

Originally published in the Jerusalem Post on January 18, 2021

HISTORICAL BACKGROUND TO THE PURIM STORY ACCORDING TO JEWISH TRADITION

Batya Markowitz

ESTHER COMES FROM THE HEBREW WORD HESTER (הסתר), WHICH means 'hidden.' *Megilla* (מגילה), 'scroll,' is related to the word *ligalot* (לגלות), which means 'to reveal.' The challenge of reading *Megillat Esther* (Esther) is to reveal the hidden messages veiled within the exciting plot. At first glance, the story seems to be one of royal intrigue, power, wealth and politics. Superficially, the events of the *Megilla* seem to be the result of the whims of an intoxicated king. The name of God does not appear even once in the entire story, making *Megillat Esther* the only book of the *Tanakh* that does not mention His holy name. The reader's job, therefore, is to uncover *Hashem*'s hidden hand guiding what appears to be a string of coincidences.

Megillat Esther contains an account of events that took place when the Jewish people were living in Persia. Following the destruction of the first *Beit Hamikdash* in 586 BCE at the hands of the Babylonians, the Jews were exiled to Babylon. Not long afterwards, the Babylonians were defeated by Cyrus, king of Persia in 539 BCE, and the Jewish residents of Babylon found themselves under Persian rule. The story of *Esther* takes place against this backdrop of Persian exile.

Cyrus the Great was the first Persian king to control Babylon. In the first year of his reign he made a famous decree, granting permission for the Jews to return to Jerusalem and rebuild their Temple (Ezra 1:1–3). Unfortunately, not many heeded the call. Though construction of the *Beit Hamikdash* begins soon after this first, small, wave of exiles returned, it is quickly halted. Not until the second year of King Darius's reign does construction of the Temple resume, and it is finally completed

in Darius's sixth year. Jewish tradition places King Ahasuerus between Cyrus and Darius. The Sages even suggest that Darius was the son of Ahasuerus and *Esther*. In their opinion, the story of *Esther* takes place after the Cyrus declaration, but before the reconstruction of the *Beit Hamikdash*. According to this opinion, the Jews of the story are the very ones who disregard the decree of Cyrus, and choose to remain in exile rather than returning to *Eretz Yisrael* to participate in the reconstruction of the Temple and *Yerushalayim*.

According to the Sages (*Megilla* 11a), Ahasuerus halted the reconstruction of the *Beit Hamikdash*, and he threw a feast when he believed that the Jews had been forsaken and would never return to *Yerushalayim*. He deliberately offered *Esther* only "half the kingdom" (Esther 5:3), refusing to restart the construction of the *Beit Hamikdash*. Meanwhile, *Mordechai*, a former citizen of *Yerushalayim* living in Shushan, the capital of the Persian Empire, was teaching about the *Beit Hamikdash* and putting aside money for its construction. At the same time, however, the Jews of the Persian Empire had weakened their connection to *Eretz Yisrael*. They could have immigrated to Israel years before during Cyrus' rule, but instead opted to remain in exile. The opening of *Megillat Esther* even finds them at Ahasuerus's feast where the Temple vessels were on display. It has been suggested that the events of the story, and the evil decree of Haman, were Divine retribution for forsaking the Land of Israel and the *Beit Hamikdash*.

The miracle of the story of *Esther* carries an important message to the people of that time, and for all ages. Living in exile, the Jews felt physically distanced from their land, and spiritually distanced from their God. They no longer deserved the open miracles they had experienced in the past in their homeland. Nevertheless, the story of *Esther* teaches that *Hashem* did not, and will not, abandon His people. Although He is hidden in exile, He is very much present, pulling the strings from behind the scenes. The God who created the world and who split the sea is the same God who deposed Vashti, chose *Esther* and hanged Haman.

In a subtle way, *Megillat Esther* reminds its readers throughout the

ages of some very fundamental ideas. First, they must never forsake *Yerushalayim*, but must remember her no matter where they find themselves. Second, even outside of Israel, where *Hashem*'s presence is less obvious, they must discover and reveal the hidden God, and must see Him in all aspects of day-to-day life, not just in open miracles. And finally, they must always remember that *Hashem* will never forsake His promise to return the Children of Israel to the Land of Israel.

PROPHETS AND PROPHETESSES OF THE HEBREW BIBLE

List of the *Neviim* (Prophets) and *Neviot* (Prophetesses)

Esther was not only a heroine of the Jewish people, but, according to the ancient Jewish Sages, she was also a prophetess. The Talmud (*Megillah* 14a) states that there were 48 prophets and 7 prophetesses in the Hebrew Bible.

The following is a list of prophets and prophetesses based on *Rashi's* enumeration, as well as the main places in *Tanakh* that they are mentioned:

The 48 *Neviim*	Biblical Reference
Avraham	Genesis 11:26–25:11
Yitzchak	Genesis 21:1–28:9
Yaakov	Genesis 25:19–50:13
Moshe	Exodus 2–Deuteronomy 34
Aharon	Exodus 4:14–Numbers 20:29
Yehoshua son of *Nun*	The Book of Joshua
Pinchas son of *Elazar*	Numbers 25:1–15
Elkana	I Samuel 1
Eli	I Samuel 1–4:18
Shmuel son of *Elkana*	I Samuel 1–25:1
Gad	I Samuel 22:5, II Samuel 24:11,19
Natan	II Samuel 7, 12, II Kings 1
David son of *Yishai*	I Samuel 15–II Kings 2:13
Achiya the Shilonite	I Kings 11:29–39, 14:1–16
Shlomo son of *David*	I Kings 2–11

The 48 Neviim	Biblical Reference
Ido	II Chronicles 12:15, 13:22
Shemaya	I Kings 12:22–24, II Chronicles 12:5–15
Eliyahu	I Kings 17:1–II Kings 2:12
Michaihu	I Kings 22
Ovadya	The Book of Obadiah
Chanani	II Chronicles 16:7–10
Yehu son of **Chanani**	I Kings 16:1–7
Azarya son of **Oded**	II Chronicles 15:1–8
Yachaziel son of **Zecharya**	II Chronicles 20:14–17
Eliezer son of **Dodavahu**	II Chronicles 20:37
Elisha son of **Shafat**	II Kings 2–9, 13:14–21
Yona son of **Amitai**	The Book of Jonah
Hoshea son of **B'eri**	The Book of Hosea
Amos	The Book of Amos
Amotz	Father of *Yeshayahu** – Isaiah 1:1
Oded	II Chronicles 28:9–11
Yeshayahu son of **Amotz**	The Book of Isaiah
Micha of **Moreshet**	The Book of Micah
Yoel son of **Petuel**	The Book of Joel
Nachum	The Book of Nahum
Uriah son of **Shemaya**	Jeremiah 26:20–23
Chavakuk	The Book of Habakkuk
Tzefanya son of **Kushi**	The Book of Zephaniah

The 48 Neviim	Biblical Reference
Yirmiyahu son of **Chilkiyahu**	The Book of Jeremiah
Yechezkel son of **Buzi**	The Book of Ezekiel
Neriya	Father of *Baruch* and *Seraya** – Jeremiah 32:12,16 36:4,8,14,32 43:3,6 45:1 51:59
Baruch son of **Neriya**	Jeremiah 32, 36, 43:2–7, 45
Seraya son of **Neriya**	Jeremiah 51:59–64
Machaseya	Father of *Neriya** – Jeremiah 32:12, 51:59
Chagai	The Book of Haggai
Zecharya	The Book of Zechariah
Malachi	The Book of Malachi
Mordechai	The Book of Esther

	The 7 Neviot
Sara	Genesis 11:29 – 23:20
Miriam	Exodus 2:1–9, 15:20–21 Numbers 12:1–15, 20:1
Devora	Judges 4–5
Chana	I Samuel 1:1–2:21
Avigail	I Samuel 25
Chulda	II Kings 22:14–20
Esther	The Scroll of Esther

NOTES ON TRANSLATION AND TRANSLITERATED WORDS

THE ISRAEL BIBLE RELIES UPON THE NEW JEWISH PUBLICATION Society translation of the Hebrew Bible. However, for the Scroll of Esther, we created our own original English translation. Translating the *Tanakh* out of its original holy language of Hebrew is by definition, an impossible task. Nevertheless, we pray that our effort provides an accurate and readable version that our readers will benefit from.

To give readers of *The Israel Bible* an authentic Hebrew experience, every verse that has our commentary is transliterated from Hebrew into English, enabling even readers who don't know Hebrew to decipher key biblical passages in the holy language. Readers can hear the entire Scroll of Esther chanted in Hebrew on our website www.TheIsraelBible.com.

In addition to whole verses, we have also transliterated many proper nouns in the English translation so that our readers can learn the names of key biblical figures and locations in their original form. As a rule, we chose to transliterate names of people that were central in the establishment and functioning of the nation of Israel, as well as significant places in the Holy Land. Therefore, *Mordechai* (Mordecai) is transliterated but Ahasuerus is not; *Yerushalayim* is transliterated, but Shushan is not.

In our commentary, we also transliterated ideas and concepts that are central to Judaism such as the *Beit Hamikdash* (Temple). Finally, the name of God, which does not appear in the text but does appear in our commentary, is transliterated. Out of respect, Orthodox Jews generally refer to the Lord as *Hashem*, which literally means 'the Name.' Referring to God as *Hashem* reminds us that we feel close to Him but also recognize our distance at the same time.

LIST OF TRANSLITERATED WORDS IN MEGILLAT ESTHER

THE FOLLOWING IS A COMPREHENSIVE LIST OF WORDS WHICH have been transliterated into Hebrew in the English translation and commentary of *Megillat Esther*

Hebrew Name	English Name	Pronunciation	Hebrew
Adar	Adar	a-DAR	אֲדָר
Amah	Cubit	a-MAH	אַמָּה
Av	Ab	av	אָב
Avichayil	Abihail	a-vee-KHA-yil	אֲבִיחַיִל
Bat	Daughter of	bat	בַּת
Beit Hamikdash	Temple	bayt ha-mik-DASH	בֵּית הַמִּקְדָּשׁ
Ben	Son of	ben	בֶּן
Binyamin	Benjamin	bin-ya-MIN	בִּנְיָמִין
Daniel	Daniel	da-ni-YAYL	דָּנִיֵּאל
Elul	Elul	e-LUL	אֱלוּל
Eretz Yisrael	Land of Israel	E-retz yis-ra-AYL	אֶרֶץ יִשְׂרָאֵל
Esther	Esther	es-TAYR	אֶסְתֵּר
Ezra	Ezra	ez-RA	עֶזְרָא
Hadassah	Hadassah	ha-da-SAH	הֲדַסָּה
Hashem	Lord/God		
Keesh	Kish	keesh	קִישׁ
Leah	Leah	lay-AH	לֵאָה
Mordechai	Mordecai	mor-d'-KHAI	מָרְדֳּכַי
Nisan	Nisan	nee-SAN	נִיסָן

List of Transliterated Words in Megillat Esther

Hebrew Name	English Name	Pronunciation	Hebrew
Pesach	Passover	PE-sakh	פֶּסַח
Pur	Lottery	pur	פּוּר
Purim	Purim	pu-REEM	פּוּרִים
Shaul	Saul	sha-UL	שָׁאוּל
Shim'i	Shimei	shim-EE	שִׁמְעִי
Sivan	Sivan	see-VAN	סִיוָן
Tevet	Tebeth	tay-VAYT	טֵבֵת
Tzefanya	Zephaniah	tz'-fan-YAH	צְפַנְיָה
Yair	Jair	ya-EER	יָאִיר
Yechonya	Jeconiah	y'-khon-YAH	יְכָנְיָה
Yehuda	Judah	y'-hu-DAH	יְהוּדָה
Yerushalayim	Jerusalem	y'-ru-sha-LA-yim	יְרוּשָׁלַיִם

THE HEBREW MONTHS AND THEIR HOLIDAYS

Jewish Month	Approximate Secular Date	Holiday	Hebrew Date	Notes
		Rosh Chodesh (Head of the Month)	The first of every month	The Jewish Calendar is a lunar calendar, and each month begins when the moon re-appears in the sky. The beginning of each new month is called *Rosh Chodesh*, which literally means 'the head of the month.' *Rosh Chodesh* is celebrated as a mini-holiday on the first day of every Jewish month, and special prayers are added into the daily service. When a month is 30 days long, the 30th day is celebrated as *Rosh Chodesh* in addition to the first day of the following month.
Nisan	March–April	*Pesach* (Passover)	Begins on the 15th of *Nisan*	*Pesach* is a seven day holiday commemorating the Exodus from Egypt. Outside of Israel, an eighth day is observed.
		Yom Hashoa (Holocaust Memorial Day)	27th of *Nisan*	*Yom Hashoa* commemorates the 6 million Jews who perished in the Holocaust.
Iyar	April–May	*Yom Hazikaron* (Memorial Day)	4th of *Iyar*	*Yom Hazikaron* is Israel's memorial day, a day to remember Israel's fallen soldiers and victims of terror.
		Yom Haatzmaut (Israel's Independence Day)	5th of *Iyar*	*Yom Haatzmaut* celebrates Israel's declaration of independence in 1948.
		Lag Ba'Omer (33rd day of the Omer)	18th of *Iyar*	*Lag Ba'Omer* is a minor holiday celebrated on the 33rd day of the counting of the Omer
		Yom Yerushalayim (Jerusalem Day)	28th of *Iyar*	*Yom Yerushalayim*, Jerusalem Day, celebrates the re-unification of the city of Jerusalem following the 1967 Six-Day War.
Sivan	May–June	*Shavuot* (Feast of Weeks)	6th of *Sivan*	*Shavuot* celebrates the giving of the *Torah* at Mount Sinai. Outside of Israel it is observed for two days, the 6th and 7th of *Sivan*.

The Hebrew Months and their Holidays

Jewish Month	Approximate Secular Date	Holiday	Hebrew Date	Notes
Tammuz	June–July	Fast of the Seventeenth of *Tammuz*	17th of *Tammuz*	The Fast of the Seventeenth of *Tammuz* commemorates the breeching of the walls of Jerusalem before the destruction of the Temple. It begins a three week mourning period over the destruction of the Temple, culminating with the fast of *Tisha B'Av*.
Av	July–August	*Tisha B'Av* (Fast of the 9th of *Av*)	9th of *Av*	*Tisha B'Av* is a fast day commemorating the destruction of the Temple in Jerusalem. It is the culmination of the three week mourning period over the destruction of the Temple which starts on the 17th of *Tammuz*.
Elul	August–September			
Tishrei	September–October	Rosh Hashana (Jewish New Year)	1st and 2nd of *Tishrei*	*Rosh Hashana* is the Jewish New Year.
		Tzom Gedalya (Fast of Gedaliah)	3rd of *Tishrei*	The Fast of Gedaliah commemorates the death of Gedaliah son of Ahikam, the governor of Judah following the destruction of the First Temple. His death marked the end of Jewish rule in the Land of Israel for many generations and led to the exile of the few remaining Jews who had not been taken to Babylonia.
		Yom Kippur (Day of Atonement)	10th of *Tishrei*	*Yom Kippur* is the Day of Atonement, the holiest day of the year.
		Sukkot (Feast of Tabernacles)	Begins on the 15th of *Tishrei*	*Sukkot* is a seven-day holiday celebrating God's protection of the Jews in the wilderness
		Shemini Atzeret/ Simchat Torah (Eighth Day of Assembly)	22nd of *Tishrei*	*Shemini Atzeret* is a holiday that immediately follows *Sukkot* and celebrates the unique relationship between God and the Children of Israel. *Simchat Torah* celebrates the completion and renewal of the *Torah* reading cycle. In Israel, *Shemini Atzeret* and *Simchat Torah* are celebrated on the same day. Outside of Israel, they are celebrated on two consecutive days.
Cheshvan	October–November			

The Hebrew Months and their Holidays

Jewish Month	Approximate Secular Date	Holiday	Hebrew Date	Notes
Kislev	November–December	*Chanukah* (Hanukkah)	Begins on the 25th of *Kislev*	*Chanukah* is an eight day festival which celebrates the defeat of the Syrian-Greeks, the re-dedication of the Temple in Jerusalem, and the miracles that God preformed to facilitate these events.
Tevet	December–January	The end of *Chanukah* (Hanukkah)	*Chanukah* ends on the 2nd or 3rd of *Tevet* depending on the year, since *Kislev* contains either 29 or 30 days	
		Fast of the 10th of *Tevet*	10th of *Tevet*	The Fast of the 10th of *Tevet* commemorates the Babylonian siege of Jerusalem prior to the destruction of the First Temple.
Shevat	January–February	*Tu B'Shvat* (15th of *Shevat*)	15th of *Shevat*	*Tu B'Shvat* marks the beginning of the new year for trees. It is when the first trees in the Land of Israel begin to blossom again after the winter season.
Adar*	February–March	Fast of Esther	13th of *Adar*	The Fast of Esther commemorates the fast observed by the Jewish people in Persia at the time of *Mordechai* and *Esther*.
		Purim	14th/15th of *Adar*	Purim celebrates God's salvation of the Jews from the evil Haman's plot to destroy them. In most places, this holiday is celebrated on the 14th of *Adar*. In Jerusalem, it is celebrated on the 15th of *Adar*.

* During a leap year, an extra month of Adar is added so that the Jewish lunar calendar remains aligned with the solar seasons. A leap year occurs 7 times in every 19 year cycle. When this happens, Purim is celebrated in the second *Adar*.

MAP OF THE EMPIRE OF AHASUERUS

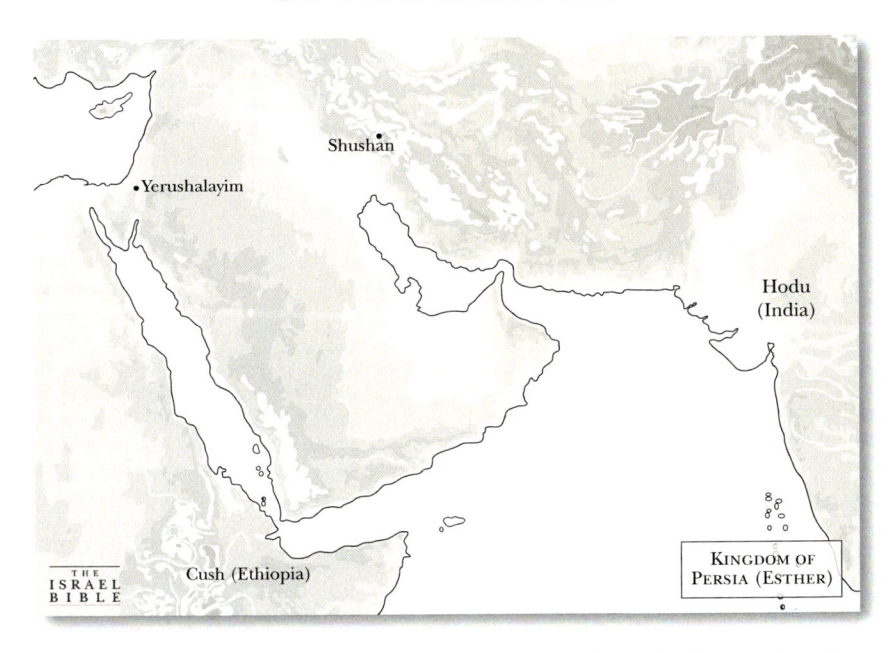

This map highlights Ahasuerus's vast empire as described in the Book of Esther (1:1–2).

1. Ahasuerus, king of Persia, ruled a vast empire from Hodu (**India**) to Cush (**Ethiopia**) (Esther 1:1).
2. **Shushan**, located in modern-day Iran, was the capital of the Persian empire (Esther 1:2). It is where the events of the Book of Esther took place.
3. *Yerushalayim*, and the entire **Land of Israel**, were part of Ahasuerus's kingdom and fell under his rule.

MAP OF MODERN DAY ISRAEL AND ITS NEIGHBORS

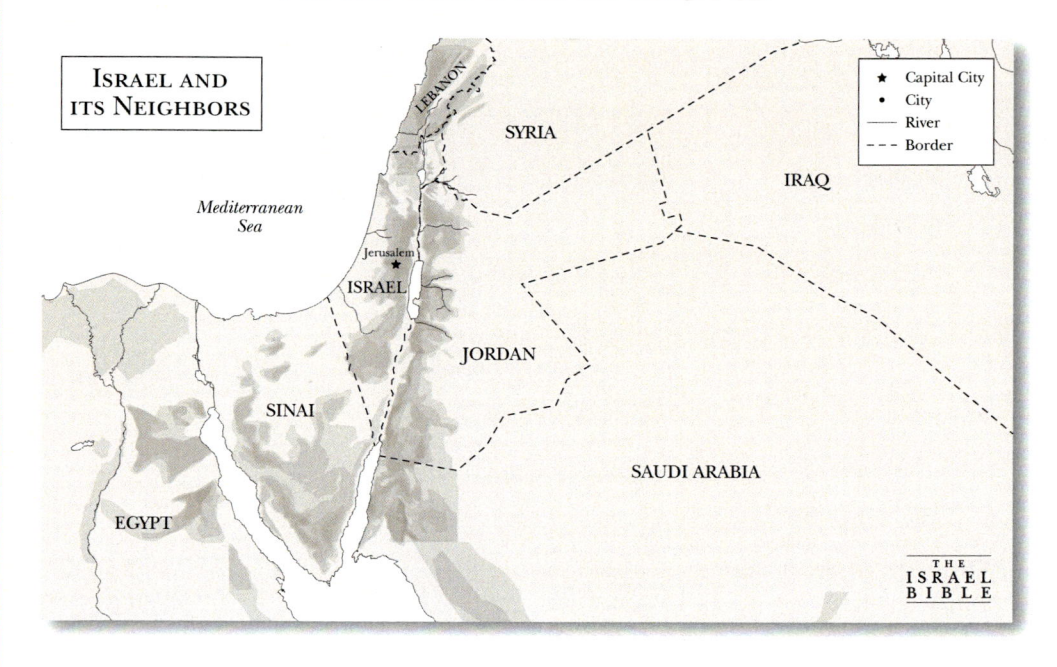

PRAYER FOR THE STATE OF ISRAEL

Our Heavenly Father	a-VEE-nu she-ba-sha-MA-yim	אָבִינוּ שֶׁבַּשָּׁמַיִם
Israel's Rock and Redeemer	tzur yis-ra-AYL v'-go-a-LO	צוּר יִשְׂרָאֵל וְגוֹאֲלוֹ
Bless the State of Israel	ba-RAYKH et mi-dee-NAT yis-ra-AYL	בָּרֵךְ אֶת מְדִינַת יִשְׂרָאֵל
the first flowering of our redemption	ray-SHEET tz'-mee-KHAT g'-u-la-TAY-nu	רֵאשִׁית צְמִיחַת גְּאֻלָּתֵנוּ
Shield it under the wings of Your loving kindness	ha-GAYN a-LE-ha b'-ev-RAT khas-DE-kha	הָגֵן עָלֶיהָ בְּאֶבְרַת חַסְדֶּךָ
And spread over it the Tabernacle of Your peace	uf-ROS a-LE-ha su-KAT sh'-lo-ME-kha	וּפְרוֹס עָלֶיהָ סֻכַּת שְׁלוֹמֶךָ
Send Your light and truth	ush-LAKH o-r'-KHA va-a-mi-t'-KHA	וּשְׁלַח אוֹרְךָ וַאֲמִתְּךָ
to its leaders, ministers and officials	l'-ro-SHE-ha, sa-RE-ha v'-yo-a-TZE-ha	לְרָאשֶׁיהָ, שָׂרֶיהָ וְיוֹעֲצֶיהָ
And direct them with good counsel before You	v'-ta-k'-NAYM b'-ay-TZAH to-VAH m'-li-fa-NE-kha	וְתַקְּנֵם בְּעֵצָה טוֹבָה מִלְּפָנֶיךָ
Strengthen the hands of the defenders of our Holy Land	kha-ZAYK et y'-DAY m'-gi-NAY E-retz kod-SHAY-nu	חַזֵּק אֶת יְדֵי מְגִנֵּי אֶרֶץ קָדְשֵׁנוּ

Grant them deliverance, our God	v'-han-khee-LAYM e-lo-HAY-nu y'-shu-AH	וְהַנְחִילֵם אֱלֹהֵינוּ יְשׁוּעָה
And crown them with the crown of victory	va-a-TE-ret ni-tza-KHON t'-a-t'-RAYM	וַעֲטֶרֶת נִצָּחוֹן תְּעַטְּרֵם
Grant peace in the land	v'-na-ta-TA sha-LOM ba-A-retz	וְנָתַתָּ שָׁלוֹם בָּאָרֶץ
and everlasting joy to its inhabitants	v'-sim-KHAT o-LAM l'-yo-sh'-VE-ha	וְשִׂמְחַת עוֹלָם לְיוֹשְׁבֶיהָ
As for our brothers, the whole house of Israel	v'-ET a-KHAY-nu kol bayt yis-ra-AYL	וְאֶת אַחֵינוּ כָּל בֵּית יִשְׂרָאֵל
Remember them in all the lands of their dispersion	p'-KOD na b'-KHOL ar-TZOT p'-zu-ray-HEM	פְּקָד נָא בְּכָל אַרְצוֹת פְּזוּרֵיהֶם
And swiftly lead them upright	v'-to-lee-KHAYM m'-hay-RAH ko-m'-mi-YUT	וְתוֹלִיכֵם מְהֵרָה קוֹמְמִיּוּת
to *Zion* Your city	l'-TZI-yon ee-RE-kha	לְצִיּוֹן עִירֶךָ
And *Yerushalayim* Your dwelling place	v'-lee-ru-sha-LA-yim mish-KAN sh'-ME-kha	וְלִירוּשָׁלַיִם מִשְׁכַּן שְׁמֶךָ
As is written in the *Torah* of *Moses* Your servant (Deut. 30:4–5):	ka-ka-TUV b'-to-RAT mo-SHEH av-DE-kha:	כַּכָּתוּב בְּתוֹרַת מֹשֶׁה עַבְדֶּךָ (דברים ל:ד-ה):
"Even if you are scattered to the furthermost lands under the heavens	"im yih-YEH ni-da-kha-KHA bik-TZAY ha-sha-MA-yim	"אִם יִהְיֶה נִדַּחֲךָ בִּקְצֵה הַשָּׁמָיִם
From there the Lord your God will gather you	mi-SHAM yi-ka-betz-KHA a-do-NAI e-lo-HE-kha	מִשָּׁם יְקַבֶּצְךָ יְיָ אֱלֹהֶיךָ

and from there He will and take you back	u-mi-SHAM yi-ka-KHE-kha	וּמִשָּׁם יִקָּחֶךָ
The Lord your God will bring you to the land	ve-he-vee-a-KHA a-do-NAI e-lo-HE-kha el ha-A-retz	וֶהֱבִיאֲךָ יְיָ אֱלֹהֶיךָ אֶל הָאָרֶץ
That your ancestors possessed	a-SHER ya-r'-SHU a-vo-TE-khe	אֲשֶׁר יָרְשׁוּ אֲבֹתֶיךָ
and you will possess it	vee-rish-TAH	וִירִשְׁתָּהּ
And He will make you more prosperous and numerous than your ancestors"	v'-hay-tiv-KHA v'-hir-b'-KHA may-a-vo-TE-kha"	וְהֵיטִבְךָ וְהִרְבְּךָ מֵאֲבֹתֶיךָ"
Unite our hearts	v'-ya-KHAYD l'-va-VAY-nu	וְיַחֵד לְבָבֵנוּ
to love and revere Your name	l'-a-ha-VAH ul-yir-AH et sh'-ME-kha	לְאַהֲבָה וּלְיִרְאָה אֶת שְׁמֶךָ
And observe all the words of Your *Torah*	v'-lish-MOR et kol div-RAY to-ra-TE-kha	וְלִשְׁמֹר אֶת כָּל דִּבְרֵי תוֹרָתֶךָ
And swiftly send us	ush-LAKH LA-nu m'-hay-RAH	וּשְׁלַח לָנוּ מְהֵרָה
Your righteous anointed one of the house of *David*	ben da-VID m'-SHEE-akh tzid-KE-kha	בֶּן דָּוִד מְשִׁיחַ צִדְקֶךָ
To redeem those who long for Your salvation	lif-DOT m'-kha-KAY kaytz y'-shu-a-TE-kha	לִפְדּוֹת מְחַכֵּי קֵץ יְשׁוּעָתֶךָ
Appear in Your glorious majesty	ho-FA ba-ha-DAR g'-ON u-ZE-kha	הוֹפַע בַּהֲדַר גְּאוֹן עֻזֶּךָ

over all the dwellers on earth	al kol yo-sh'-VAY TAY-vayl ar-TZE-kha	עַל כָּל יוֹשְׁבֵי תֵבֵל אַרְצֶךָ
And let all who breathe declare:	v'-yo-MAR kol a-SHER n'-sha-MAH v'-a-PO	וְיֹאמַר כֹּל אֲשֶׁר נְשָׁמָה בְאַפּוֹ
The Lord God of Israel is King	a-do-NAI e-lo-HAY yis-ra-AYL ME-lekh	יְיָ אֱלֹהֵי יִשְׂרָאֵל מֶלֶךְ
And His kingship has dominion over all	u-mal-khu-TO ba-KOL ma-sha-LAH,	וּמַלְכוּתוֹ בַּכֹּל מָשָׁלָה
Amen, Selah	a-MAYN SE-lah	אָמֵן סֶלָה

PRAYER FOR THE WELFARE OF ISRAEL'S SOLDIERS

He Who blessed our forefathers	mee she-bay-RAKH a-vo-TAY-nu	מִי שֶׁבֵּרַךְ אֲבוֹתֵינוּ
Avraham, Yitzchak and Yaakov	av-ra-HAM yitz-KHAK v'-ya-a-KOV	אַבְרָהָם יִצְחָק וְיַעֲקֹב
may He bless the fighters of the Israel Defense Forces	hu y'-va-RAYKH et kha-ya-LAY tz'-VA ha-ha-ga-NAH l'-yis-ra-AYL	הוּא יְבָרֵךְ אֶת חַיְלֵי צְבָא הַהֲגָנָה לְיִשְׂרָאֵל
and the security personnel	v'-an-SHAY ko-KHOT ha-bi-ta-KHON	וְאַנְשֵׁי כֹּחוֹת הַבִּטָּחוֹן
who stand guard over our land	ha-o-m'-DEEM al mish-MAR ar-TZAY-nu	הָעוֹמְדִים עַל מִשְׁמַר אַרְצֵנוּ
and the cities of our God	v'-a-RAY e-lo-HAY-nu	וְעָרֵי אֱלֹהֵינוּ
from the border of the Lebanon to the desert of Egypt	mi-g'-VUL ha-l'-va-NON v'-AD mid-BAR mitz-RA-yim	מִגְּבוּל הַלְּבָנוֹן וְעַד מִדְבַּר מִצְרַיִם
and from the Great Sea unto the approach of the Aravah	u-MIN ha-YAM ha-ga-DOL ad l'-VO ha-a-ra-VAH	וּמִן הַיָּם הַגָּדוֹל עַד לְבוֹא הָעֲרָבָה
on the land, in the air, and on the sea	ba-ya-ba-SHAH ba-a-VEER u-va-YAM	בַּיַּבָּשָׁה בָּאֲוִיר וּבַיָּם
May the Almighty cause the enemies who rise up against us	yi-TAYN a-do-NAI et o-y'-VAY-nu ha-ka-MEEM a-LAY-nu	יִתֵּן יְיָ אֶת אוֹיְבֵינוּ הַקָּמִים עָלֵינוּ
to be struck down before them	ni-ga-FEEM lif-nay-HEM	נִגָּפִים לִפְנֵיהֶם

Prayer for the Welfare of Israel's Soldiers

English	Transliteration	Hebrew
May the Holy One, Blessed is He	ha-ka-DOSH ba-RUKH hu	הַקָּדוֹשׁ בָּרוּךְ הוּא
preserve and rescue our fighters	yish-MOR v'-ya-TZEEL et kha-ya-LAY-nu	יִשְׁמֹר וְיַצִּיל אֶת חַיָלֵינוּ
from every trouble and distress	mi-KOL tza-RAH v'-tzu-KAH	מִכָּל צָרָה וְצוּקָה
and from every plague and illness	u-mi-KOL NE-ga u-ma-kha-LAH	וּמִכָּל נֶגַע וּמַחֲלָה
and may He send blessing and success	v'-yish-LAKH b'-ra-KHAH v'-hatz-la-KHAH	וְיִשְׁלַח בְּרָכָה וְהַצְלָחָה
in their every endeavor	b'-KHOL ma-a-SAY y'-day-HEM	בְּכָל מַעֲשֵׂה יְדֵיהֶם
May He lead our enemies under our soldiers' sway	yad-BAYR so-n'-AY-nu takh-tay-HEM	יַדְבֵּר שׂוֹנְאֵינוּ תַּחְתֵּיהֶם
and glorify our forces with the crown of salvation	vee-a-t'-RAYM b'-KHE-ter y'-shu-AH	וִיעַטְרֵם בְּכֶתֶר יְשׁוּעָה
and the mantle of victory	uv-a-TE-ret ni-tza-KHON	וּבַעֲטֶרֶת נִצָּחוֹן
And may there be fulfilled for them the verse (Deuteronomy 20:4):	vee-ku-YAM ba-HEM ha-ka-TUV:	וִיקֻיַּם בָּהֶם הַכָּתוּב (דברים כ,ד):
"For it is the Lord your God, Who goes with you	"kee a-do-NAI e-lo-hay-KHEM ha-ho-LAYKH i-ma-KHEM	"כִּי יְיָ אֱלֹהֵיכֶם הַהֹלֵךְ עִמָּכֶם
to battle your enemies for you	l'-hi-la-KHAYM la-KHEM im o-y'-vay-KHEM	לְהִלָּחֵם לָכֶם עִם אֹיְבֵיכֶם
to save you"	l'-ho-SHEE-a et-KHEM"	לְהוֹשִׁיעַ אֶתְכֶם"
Now let us say: Amen	v'-no-MAR "a-MAYN"	וְנֹאמַר: "אָמֵן"

HATIKVAH

As long as in the heart, within	kol od ba-lay-VAV p'-NEE-mah	כֹּל עוֹד בַּלֵּבָב פְּנִימָה
A Jewish soul still yearns	NE-fesh y'-hu-DEE ho-mi-YAH	נֶפֶשׁ יְהוּדִי הוֹמִיָּה
And onward, towards the ends of the east	ul-fa-a-TAY miz-RAKH ka-DEE-mah	וּלְפַאֲתֵי מִזְרָח, קָדִימָה
An eye still gazes toward Zion	A-yin l'-tzi-YON tzo-fi-YAH	עַיִן לְצִיּוֹן צוֹפִיָּה
Our hope is not yet lost	od lo av-DAH tik-va-TAY-nu	עוֹד לֹא אָבְדָה תִּקְוָתֵנוּ
The hope two thousand years old	ha-tik-VAH bat sh'-NOT al-PA-yim	הַתִּקְוָה בַּת שְׁנוֹת אַלְפַּיִם
To be a free nation in our land	lih-YOT am khof-SHEE b'-ar-TZAY-nu	לִהְיוֹת עַם חָפְשִׁי בְּאַרְצֵנוּ
The Land of Zion and Yerushalayim	E-retz tzi-YON vee-ru-sha-LA-yim	אֶרֶץ צִיּוֹן וִירוּשָׁלַיִם

ABOUT RABBI TULY WEISZ AND ISRAEL365

RABBI TULY WEISZ IS THE FOUNDER OF ISRAEL365 AND EDITOR of *The Israel Bible,* leading a team of Torah scholars in producing the world's first *Tanakh* to highlight the special relationship between the Land and People of Israel. Rabbi Weisz attended Yeshiva University (BA), the Rabbi Isaac Elchanan Theological Seminary (Rabbinic Ordination) and the Benjamin Cardozo School of Law (JD). Before moving to Israel in 2011, Rabbi Weisz served at the Beth Jacob Congregation in Columbus, Ohio for five years. Rabbi Tuly lives with his wife Abby and their children in Ramat Beit Shemesh, Israel.

The Israel Bible is the flagship publishing initiative of Israel365, which promotes the Jewish State through a variety of innovative platforms. Through its popular email newsletters, social media pages and websites Israel365.com, TheIsraelBible.com and Israel365news.com, Israel365 is the daily connection to Israel for millions of Jewish and Christian Zionists around the world. The Israel365 Charity Fund channels that grassroots advocacy into meaningful support for Holocaust Survivors, IDF lone soldiers, the poor and needy and other important projects throughout Israel.

Connect to Israel on a deeper level with *The Israel Bible*
The only Bible highlighting the special relationship between the Land and People of Israel. Through traditional and contemporary Jewish sources, *The Israel Bible* presents God's eternal and unchanging love for the Promised Land and His Chosen People from biblical times until today.

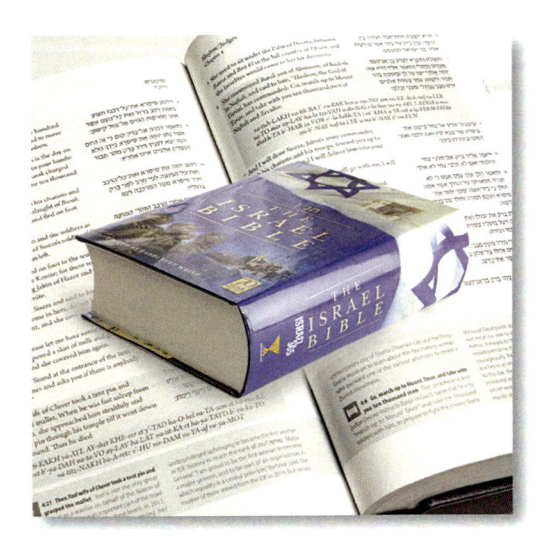

- 2,200 pages of side by side Hebrew and English
- Exclusive collection of maps, photos, charts and illustrations
- Hundreds of unique and inspiring study notes

Get your copy today at:
www.TheIsraelBible.com

THE ESTHER HORGEN MEMORIAL FOREST AND PARK

Proceeds from the sale of this volume will go to developing the Esther Horgen Memorial Forest and Park in Tal Menashe, near the site where Esther was murdered.

Upon concluding the week of mourning for their beloved Esther, the Horgen family went immediately to the site of her brutal murder in the nearby forest, and planted a tree in her memory. For the Jewish People, planting trees in the Land of Israel has always been a Biblical commandment and a symbolic act deepening our roots into the soil of our homeland as it says, "And I will plant them upon their soil, nevermore to be uprooted from the soil I have given them, said *Hashem* your God" (Amos 9:15).

Help beautify the Biblical Heartland by creating
an everlasting memorial to Esther Horgen.
To donate, please visit:
www.Israel365.com/Esther-Horgen-Memorial

For more inspiring commentary,
interactive maps, educational videos,
vivid photographs and more,
please visit our website

www.TheIsraelBible.com

THE
ISRAEL
BIBLE